A GUIDE TO FOREST HOLIDAYS
IN GREAT BRITAIN AND IRELAND

A Guide to Forest Holidays in Great Britain and Ireland

Warwick Deal

David & Charles
Newton Abbot   London
North Pomfret (VT)   Vancouver

ISBN 0 7153 7180 0
Library of Congress Catalog Card Number 76-8626
© Warwick Deal 1976

Set in 11 on 13 point Bembo
and printed in Great Britain
by Redwood Burn Limited
for David & Charles (Publishers) Limited
Brunel House Newton Abbot Devon
Published in the United States of America
by David & Charles Inc
North Pomfret Vermont 05053 USA
Published in Canada
by Douglas David & Charles Limited
1875 Welch Street North Vancouver BC

Contents

Preface

The primeval forest is the cradle from which all humanity emerged and, from time to time, there exists in every man, woman and child an inborn urge to return to the woods and trees. Until recently this need could be satisfied only by the fortunate few. Not very many forests and woodlands, whether in private or state hands, actively catered for the public. But the situation is changing rapidly.

For example, in 1964 there were no set picnic places on any of the Forestry Commission's several hundred forests scattered over the length and breadth of England, Scotland and Wales. Five years later there were 104. In a further five years the number had more than trebled to 315. In 1969 there were 92 forest trails. By 1974 there were 381. Forestry Commission campsites clocked up 586,200 camper nights in 1964. Ten years on, the number had risen to 1,217,420. So great is the demand that the Commission plans to double the number of its campsites within a decade from now. Other recreational facilities and aids, such as forest-cabin sites, information centres, nature hides and observation towers, and forest scenic drives are also multiplying fast. The Forestry Commission, the Forest and Wildlife Service of Eire, the Forestry Division of Ulster, the National Trust, county councils and private landowners are throwing open more and more gates each year to the ever-growing throng of holidaymakers and day trippers who are discovering for themselves an experience that is at once almost as old as the hills and yet brand new!

Recreational facilities which have so far become available include walking and trailing, climbing, riding, swimming, boating, canoeing, sailing, skiing, fishing, shooting and deer stalking; and for those seeking a more educational form of holiday there exist opportunities for the study of natural history, the photographing and sound recording of the woodland wildlife, or the painting and sketching of the woodland scene.

There is hardly a county in the whole of the United Kingdom and Eire which does not possess at least one – and some, very many more – forest park or other holiday forest whose woods are open to the public for relaxation, recreation or study; although, as is to be expected with so much money invested, the production of timber still remains the primary reason for their existence.

With most families now enjoying three weeks' holiday or more a year there is a marked trend towards taking a second break amidst rural or silvan surroundings. While longer holidays, coupled with wider car-ownership, substantially account for the rise in popularity of forest recreation, it is also true that an increasing number of one-holiday-per-annum families are showing a preference for forest holidays over other kinds. And there is, as well, a move towards multi-purpose holidays in which forests either become ports of call on a touring holiday, or the holiday is split between, say, forest and seaside.

For easy reference, this book is divided into three parts. In Part A you will find my own selection of holiday forests, as well as the means of discovering others which may prove better suited to your needs. Part B describes the very wide range of sporting activities, recreational amenities and educational pursuits open to you on a forest holiday in the British Isles, and lists sources from which information can be obtained concerning them, including what is offered by which forests. Part C deals with the suitability and availability of the various types of forest and near-forest accommodation. You will find all the facts you need to plan what should be an enjoyable and memorable forest holiday.

NOTE

The views expressed in this book are entirely my own and are in no way to be interpreted as those of the Forestry Commission with which body I served.

Main Forest Parks and Key Holiday Forests in the British Isles

PART A

Choosing Your Holiday Forest

Introduction

Very few people in the British Isles live more than an hour or so's drive from one kind of holiday forest or another. Day and half-day trips to the woods where amenities and a range of interests are laid on are therefore open to almost anyone who has the means to travel. Those holiday forests which lend themselves to longer stays are fewer – although still sufficiently plentiful – than those which cater for day visitors only; so it will often be necessary to look farther afield for these.

Holiday forests are broadly of two main kinds: the forest park and the leisure or recreational forest. With both these types visitor amenities and facilities have been set up and, in very many cases, overnight accommodation is provided on the spot. There are also those forests, in public and private hands, which have not yet developed or begun to develop recreational facilities, and whose objects of management are still restricted to the production of timber and perhaps, as well, to the raising and pursuit of winged or ground game. Even so, many of these – or parts of them anyway – are open to the general public for the purposes of relaxation, walking and nature study.

The forest parks of England, Scotland and Wales (run by the Forestry Commission) need to be singled out for special mention. A park of this type is in reality a group of forests that have expanded towards each other or merged together in mountainous, hilly or other such kind of country with scenic appeal – the whole making an attractive holiday area in which the tree is the dominant feature. The forests and woodlands are interspersed with farmland, moorland, mountain peaks, lochs, lakes, rivers and inlets according to the park's geographical location and setting.

In Ireland, both north and south, the concept of a forest park is quite different from that of Great Britain, and it is almost always a single forest or, often, only a part of one, having a wider range of recreational facilities than a normal woodland area. The average size of a forest park in Britain is 53,000 acres plus. In Ireland it rarely exceeds 1,000 acres and is often considerably smaller. This is not to say that you will enjoy a forest park in Ireland any the less; some are exquisitely beautiful. You just need to remember that the name means two entirely different things on either side of the Irish sea.

Here, then, in this section, is my selection of holiday forests covering the whole of the British Isles. Take it only as a guide. There are lots of others for you to discover for yourself.

1 England and Wales

There is a reasonably even distribution of holiday forests of one kind and another over England and Wales. If mountainous areas with plenty of opportunity for hill-walking are what you have in mind then you will need to choose Wales or one of the northern English counties. The more gently undulating terrain, with its higher preponderance of broadleaved trees and lusher plant growth, in which to saunter or just relax, is more likely to be found in the southern half of England. Devon and Cornwall, with their hills and high moors, are exceptions; but, there, forest recreation is still, as yet, on a small scale. Generally, the northern and Welsh forests have heavier stockings of coniferous trees than broadleaved ones. But these are only rough guides. What can safely be said is that no two forests are ever quite alike. They have something to please everyone.

The Dean and Wye Valley Forest Park
Location and setting

This is a fitting holiday forest with which to begin, being set partly in England and partly in Wales, its 55 square miles extending into the three counties of Gloucestershire, Herefordshire and Monmouthshire. Its hub is the royal and ancient Forest of Dean which lies in that triangle of land where the Wye runs down to meet the Severn; but it also includes woodlands around Ross-on-Wye, Monmouth and Chepstow, and the Tintern and Chepstow Forests west of the Wye in Monmouthshire.

Established as a forest park as long ago as 1938, and in some of the most beautiful country the shires have to offer, its amenities and facilities are well planned and wide ranging. Every forest ride and woodland path throughout the Dean, Tidenham Chase, Tintern and Chepstow (the principal woodlands that comprise the forest park) is open to the public. And there are no fewer than twelve way-marked forest walks and trails, each with a written guide.

The Dean and Wye Valley Forest Park includes such spectacular scenery as the Wye Valley Gorge and Symond's Yat, and the historic buildings of Tintern Abbey, Goodrich and Chepstow castles, and the Speech House Hotel. Within easy motoring distance are the towns of Gloucester, Hereford, Newport and Monmouth. Within the park itself are Coleford, Cinderford, Lydney and Ross-on-Wye.

How to get there

Approach to the Dean and Wye Valley Forest Park from the south and east is via the M4, leaving it at junction 22 (all motorway junctions are shown on AA maps); from the north through Gloucester, Hereford or the Ross Spur Motorway (M50), leaving it at junctions 3 or 4; and from Wales via the M4, leaving it at junctions 23 or 22, or through Chepstow or Monmouth. There is no public railway through the forest park, the nearest stations being Ross-on-Wye, Lydney and Chepstow which touch upon it, or Gloucester. Bus services connect with these stations and link up most villages within the park.

Forests which comprise the park

The Forest of Dean itself, some 22,000 acres in extent, is a survivor from the even larger, primeval, deciduous, broadleaved forest which was roughly bounded by the Severn and Wye Rivers and the Malvern Hills to the north. None of it is now virgin woodland, but although there has been much planting of exotic conifers throughout the present century, the general impression is still very much that of a broadleaved or mixed forest with oak predominating.

The other four forests: Tintern, Chepstow, Tidenham Chase and Highmeadow Woods – some 13,000 acres in all – clothe and adorn the slopes of the Wye Valley and its gorge from Chepstow in the south to Symond's Yat in the north. The visitor should note, however, that not all the woodlands along the valley are publicly owned or are necessarily part of the park. Those in private hands may or may not provide public access. Again, it is the broadleaved trees which dominate the forest scene.

Plant life

The variety of plant species within the park is profuse. Main broad-leaved trees and shrubs are oak, sweet chestnut, sycamore, beech, ash, lime, birch, yew, white beam, hornbeam, field maple, privet, hawthorn, blackthorn and the service and wayfaring trees. Coniferous species include European and Japanese larches, Norway and Sitka spruce, Scots and Corsican pines, Douglas fir, Western red cedar and Western hemlock.

All the species of coniferous trees are introductions and, with the exception of Scots pine, all from overseas. These are crop trees; that is, they are being grown for commercial use. A number of broadleaved species, such as sweet chestnut and sycamore, are foreign, too. These, as well as oak, beech and ash, when in plantations, are being grown for timber. Outside, as with the other broadleaved trees and shrubs mentioned above, they are growing naturally – that is, in common with the numerous grasses, mosses, ferns and herbaceous plants, they have selected their own habitats.

That is a great feature of the Dean and Wye Valley Forest Park, its wide range of habitats – from low-lying tidal streamsides, through fertile slopes to windswept heaths almost a thousand feet above sea level. Such diversity is encouraged and multiplied by the several different types of limestone and sandstone parent rock which go to make up the various soils.

On the limestone soils you will find dog's mercury, wood anemone, bluebell, bramble, wild rose, hart's tongue fern, garlic, woodruff, rock rose, thyme and, more rarely, toothwort and stinking hellebore. On the Coal Measure Sandstones and clays of the Old Red Sandstone soils are gorse, bracken, ling and bell heather, bilberry, sheep's sorrel, heath bedstraw and numerous grasses (on the heaths); sphagnum moss, bog asphodel and sundew (in the bogs), and foxglove, rose-bay willow herb, St John's wort, marsh plume thistle, milkwort, greater stitchwort, tormentil, yellow pimpernel and speedwell (in the forest undergrowth, rides and glades). This is, by no means, an exhaustive inventory. The forest park is also prolific in its range of ferns, fungi and grasses.

Wildlife

The forest park, by virtue of its size, its range of climates and micro-climates, and its great variety of plant species, constitutes an important sanctuary for wildlife. Admittedly, there are no rarities among the mammals, but they are certainly present in telling numbers. The bear, the lynx and the auroch, the great Irish deer, the beaver and wolf and wild boar, all of which once roamed the primeval forest, have long since departed, but the fox, badger, otter, grey squirrel, hedgehog, mole, vole, long-tailed field mouse and shrew are well established. Stoats and weasels also make their appearance, but are not numerous due to the small rabbit population – their principal diet. Deer, mainly fallow, have their quarters in High Meadow.

The full range of southern species of birds are to be found within the forest park. Ravens, unknown in the locality for many years, have reappeared. The red-backed shrike – which stores the insects it catches by impaling them on thorns – is a breeding species. Among the summer visitors are garden warblers, whitethroats, chiff-chaffs, willow wrens (in large numbers), redstarts and spotted fly-catchers. The pied fly-catcher, hitherto a summer visitor, now breeds there. The nightingale is common in the Wye Valley area, but less so in the Dean Forest itself. Haw-finches can be seen among the hornbeam trees in autumn, at which time the ring doves (wood pigeons) and stock doves can be observed feeding on the acorns.

Adders, grass snakes, slow worms, lizards, toads, frogs and newts are domiciled in one part of the forest park or another. Among the bat population, the noctule abounds and the long-eared bat is plentiful; but the pipistrelle, normally the commonest bat in Britain, is some-what rare there, as is the barbastelle, while the whiskered bat and the lesser horse-shoe bat (the cave lover) are truly rare.

All these forest creatures, as well as the insects which are too numerous to mention, are listed and described in the *Dean and Wye Valley Forest Park Guide*, available from HMSO and the Forestry Commission (Coleford address, see page 21).

Places to stay

Campsites. There are two large Class A and one Class B (see page 115 for definition of site classes) campsites within the forest park. One Class A site is at Christchurch and lies on the west side of the Coleford-Symond's Yat road (B4432). The turn-off is about one mile north of Coleford and well signposted with international camping signs. An attraction of this site is that it has an extension into the adjoining woodlands and is, in fact, separately classified as a Woodland Site (see page 115). It has individual pitches among the trees. The other Class A site is at Bracelands and, although not more than four or five hundred yards away from the first, has the added bonus of fine views over the River Wye. The Class B site is at Worcester Lodge.

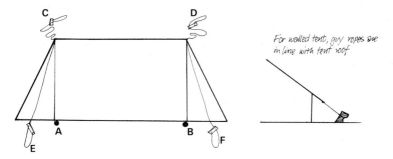

Fig 1 Weather is unpredictable and it is useful to be able to erect a tent
quickly. With a new one, practise at home beforehand. Always choose firm,
well drained ground. Open the tent so that it lies flat on the ground and insert
poles with bottom ends in positions they are to occupy when tent is upright
(points A and B in the sketch). Estimate position of pegs and tap lightly into
ground at an angle of 45° with the mallet. Attach guy ropes to pegs C and D.
Adjust position of pegs if necessary. Guy ropes to pegs E and F probably will
not reach until tent is erected. Pull steadily on guy ropes to pegs E and F –
two campers are better than one – until poles are vertical. Adjust positions of
pegs E and F if guy ropes still do not reach. Lightly and evenly tighten guy
ropes all round. Inspect to ensure that pegs are symmetrically positioned
around the tent, that poles are vertical from all angles, and that the ridge of
the tent is taut. If not, make further adjustments, then tighten guy ropes.
Slacken them a little before going to bed or leaving the site in damp or wet
weather

Bookings for these sites should be made at the Christchurch campsite on arrival. The address is: Forest Park Camp, Christchurch,
Coleford, Gloucestershire (it is shown as Berry Hill on the Ordnance
Survey maps) and the grid reference is SO 569129. For bank holiday
periods only, bookings should be made at least 14 days in advance to
the Forestry Commission, 'Camping', Crown Office, Coleford,
Gloucestershire GL16 8BA.

For private caravan and camping sites in and around the Dean and
Wye Valley Forest Park, write for the accommodation guide, *Where
to Stay in the Heart of England* (for which a charge is made), from
Dept EH, Heart of England Tourist Board, PO Box 15, Worcester
WR1 1BR.

Youth hostels. There are four youth hostels in the park: at Chepstow
(Mountain Road), Mitcheldean (Lion House), St Briavels (The Castle)
and Welsh Bicknor (The Rectory). For further information write to

Youth Hostels Association, Trevelyan House, 8 St Stephen's Hill, St Albans, Hertfordshire ALI 2DY.

Other accommodation. Hotels and guesthouses can be found at Chepstow, Cinderford, Coleford, Littledean, Lydney, Monmouth, Newnham, Ross-on-Wye, Symond's Yat and Tintern. See *Where to Stay in the Heart of England* (address above). For general accommodation guides see Part C, Chapter 2. Private house bed-and-breakfast accommodation can be obtained in any of the above places, as well as in many of the smaller villages.

For particulars of Forestry Commission holiday cottages in the Dean and Wye Valley Forest Park, write to Forestry Commission, Crown Office, Coleford, Gloucestershire, GL16 8BA. The Wye Valley and Royal Forest of Dean Tourist Board, Ross-on-Wye, Herefordshire is another useful body to contact. Ask for their accommodation list and their priced publication, *The Wyedean Guide*, which is well illustrated as well as being informative.

Holiday pursuits

Forest walks and nature trails. A great deal can be learned concerning the forest park, its wildlife, geology and history, by taking to the waymarked walks and nature trails with printed guide in hand. There are twelve of these and the more you cover the wider and deeper will become your appreciation and understanding. Armed with this information, the rest of the forest park – remember that all rides and paths are open to the public – becomes that much more pleasurable and interesting. All the walks and trails are briefly listed in *See Your Forests* (*Southern England*) – from the Forestry Commission or from the warden at the Christchurch campsite – together with their respective grid references and printed guide prices. Six are more fully described in *Nature Trails in England*, published by the English Tourist Board, 4 Grosvenor Gardens, London SW1W 0DU.

There is also a magnificent scenic circular walk of about 12 miles around the Highmeadow woods that passes, and can be broken into at, the Christchurch campsite. Average time taken is about six hours. Stout footwear is needed – not to mention willing feet. Along this walk there are some fine views over the Forest of Dean, down the Wye Gorge and up to Symond's Yat and – on a clear day – over the whole of Monmouthshire and towards the Brecon Beacons in Wales.

This walk is described in more detail in the *Short Guide to the Dean and Wye Valley Forest Park.*

Eleven other walks – not to be confused with the nature trails – are included in the *Dean and Wye Valley Forest Park Guide* (the full guide); both are obtainable from HMSO and the Forestry Commission (Coleford address, see page 21).

Maps. On these longer, and mostly unmarked, walks and for exploring generally, a map on a scale of not less than 1 in to the mile becomes essential. The Ordnance Survey (Tourist Edition) 1 in to the mile map, Wye Valley and Lower Severn, covers the whole region. But the excellent $2\frac{1}{2}$ in OS maps show many more paths – all that are known to them – in far greater detail.

Picnic sites. There are five picnic sites: at Speech House near Cinderford; Edge End near Coleford; Beechenhurst at Cannop, and two in the Tintern Forest (Monmouthshire). These are listed with grid references in *See Your Forests* (*Southern England*).

Fishing. Game fishing in the Wye is reserved, but coarse fishing is available. A licence must be obtained from the Wye River Board Fishing Office, Wilson's Chambers, Commercial Street, Hereford. In addition, permits are needed from the local owners. These are secured via the Hereford Angling Association, the Ross Angling Association and the Royal Hotel at Symond's Yat. Pond fishing within the forest park comes under the Dean Angling Club. Addresses are in the local telephone directory.

Boating. Boats are for hire at Ross and Symond's Yat on the River Wye.

Places to visit

Tintern Abbey. Cistercian, founded 1131. On the Chepstow to Monmouth Road (A466) between the road and the River Wye. Note the absence of large towers which were forbidden by the Cistercian order.

Symond's Yat Rock. One mile off the A40 on the Coleford Road. 'Yat' is believed to be a corruption of 'gate'. Magnificent views of the River Wye (including the great loop) and limestone crags. Forestry Commission car park and refreshment pavilion built on log-cabin principle with Western red cedar; roof shingles imported from Canada. Splendid walks through the woods. Ferry crosses the river at Symond's Yat (1½ miles from the Rock).

The Speech House. A pleasing example of Restoration architecture. On the Coleford to Cinderford road, 2 miles west of Cinderford. Built by Charles II in 1680. The old centre of Dean Forest administration and the Verderers Court which still meets there. The Speech House is now a hotel, but its Verderers Hall is open to visitors at any reasonable hour. The Hall is also used as a dining room, and a meal there could well be a memorable holiday experience. For the open air enthusiasts, there is a picnic site close by to the east.

Bream Village. Turn off the A48 (Chepstow to Gloucester road) at Lydney, then 3 miles. Breathtaking view over the heart of the Dean Forest from the war memorial. In nearby Lydney Park Woods are the famous Scowles where iron ore was dug in Roman times.

Goodrich Castle. On the Monmouth to Ross road (A40) at Goodrich. First mentioned in 1101 or 1102 but earliest remains are 13th century. Association with Edward I and the Welsh conquest. Last inhabited in 16th century.

King Arthur's Cave. In Lord's Wood near Whitchurch on the Monmouth to Ross road (A40). Many interesting relics of prehistoric life in the region.

Offa's Dyke (southern end). Runs parallel to and east of the Chepstow to Monmouth road (A466), roughly between Whitebrook and Llandogo, also north of Tintern. Believed to have been constructed by King Offa to divide his Mercian kingdom from Wales.

Roman Road. A major Roman road used to run from Mitcheldean through Lydney and on to Caerwent (the legionary fortress of Venta Silurum) which lies outside the forest park to the south. A section of the Roman Road can be seen near Blackpool Bridge north west of Blakeney on the Blakeney to Parkend road.

Cannop Ponds. This is a mile-long stretch of water well stocked with coarse fish, ornamental water fowl, and fringed with oak and beech, lying about ¾ mile south of Cannop. It has a picnic site – grid reference: SO 608105.

Publications

Other useful publications – priced unless otherwise stated – are:
Dean Visitor Map
A Scenic Motor Drive through the Dean Forest Park

The address from which to obtain these, and other Forestry Commission publications mentioned in this section, is: Forestry Commission, Crown Office, Coleford, Gloucestershire GL16 8BA.

Snowdonia Forest Park
Location and setting

This is a forest park (established in 1937) within a national park (Snowdonia National Park, established in 1951); but whereas most of the land within the wider boundaries of the national park is not, contrary to its title, nationally owned, most of that lying inside the forest park is. Snowdonia Forest Park is made up of two forests, Beddgelert to the west of Mount Snowdon (3,561 ft), and Gwydyr to the east. Together they amount to some 23,000 acres of woodlands, with a further 5,000 acres added for lakes and moorland. The main area, Gwydyr Forest, lies on the western slopes of the Conway Valley and in the smaller valleys and on the higher ground around, taking Betws y Coed (on the A470) as its north-south centre. The smaller area, Beddgelert Forest, is to the north of the village from which it derives its name (on the A487) and occupies part of the watershed between the Afon Gwyrfai – 'river that winds' – and the Afon Colwyn – 'river of the cubs'. The famous Lleyn Peninsula to the west of the forest park, and the towns of Caernarvon, Bangor, Llandudno, Colwyn Bay and Portmadog are all within easy motoring distance.

How to get there

Approaches by road are: via Chester (for those coming from the north) taking the A55, the A541 and the A543 (to Pentrefoelas), and thence via the A5 (heading north-west) to Betws y Coed; via Shrewsbury (for those from the Midlands and the south) taking the A5 direct to Betws y Coed.

By rail: leave the London-Chester-Holyhead line at Llandudno Junction and entrain for Betws y Coed. There is no railway line to the Beddgelert section of the forest park – nearest stations are

(Plate 1 overleaf) Riding in Snowdonia Forest Park, Lake Gerionydd in the background *(Forestry Commission)*

Portmadog and Caernarvon, 8 and 12 miles away, respectively. The bus services within the forest park and in the surrounding region are good, but very few routes operate on Sundays.

Plant life

The planted woodlands, particularly in the Conway Valley section, consist of impressive stands of firs, spruces, larches and pines on the plateaux and clinging to the hillsides, with broadleaved trees of oak, beech, sycamore and poplar in the more fertile valleys. The natural woodlands, small in extent, are mainly of scrub and coppice oak, with some beech, birch and alder. Plant life is of great variety and, although there are no rarities, of considerable interest to the botanist. The widely known – though small – arctic/alpine communities are outside the boundaries of the forest park, but close by in the corries and cwms of Snowdon, Glyders and other mountains. Within the park the plant life ranges in habitat from streamsides, lakes, fields, woodlands (broadleaved and coniferous), fells, peat bogs, heather moors, scree and crag.

Wildlife

With such diversity of habitat and vegetation, the wildlife, as may be expected, is also very varied. Birds include a number of the warblers, pied flycatcher, nightjar, redstart, woodcock, woodpeckers, whinchat, stonechat, dipper, curlew, buzzard, raven and ring ouzel. The local celebrities in the mammal world are the polecat and the pine marten, which belong to the same family as the stoat, weasel, otter and badger; these are also present, but have much more restricted habitats. The three principal species of British voles are common, so also are the long-tailed field mouse (which, when caught by its tail, can break it off and escape); the common shrew, and the pigmy or lesser shrew. The water shrew is less common and more localised. There are at least seven species of bat: the noctule, pipistrelle, long-eared, whiskered, Daubenton's, Natterer's and lesser horseshoe. Reptiles include the adder, grass snake (Britain's largest) and several lizards. Among the amphibians are the palmate and warty newts, and the common frog and toad. Coarse fish are surprisingly scarce, but salmon, sea and brown trout are plentiful.

Places to stay

Campsites. The Forestry Commission has a large and very well-laid-out Class A caravan and camping site at Beddgelert Forest. It stands at the very foot of Snowdon close to the start of the Rhyd Ddu and Beddgelert tracks to the summit, which is about 3 miles away. The campsite is about a mile north of Beddgelert village on the road to Caernarvon (A487). The turn-off is to the left. Grid reference: SH 578491. Address: The Warden, Snowdonia Forest Park Camp, Beddgelert, Caernarvonshire. A limited number of places are reserved for advanced bookings for the Easter and Spring bank holidays, and for a period of seven days or more throughout the season, which lasts from 1 April (or Easter, if earlier) to 30 September. Applications for advanced bookings should be made 14 days in advance to the Forestry Commission, Beddgelert. Caernarvonshire, LL55 4UU.

The National Trust, 42 Queen Anne's Gate, London SW1H 9AS has three campsites within the eastern section (Gwydyr Forest): Carnedd, Gwerngof, Isaf, Capel Curig (tents but no caravans), grid

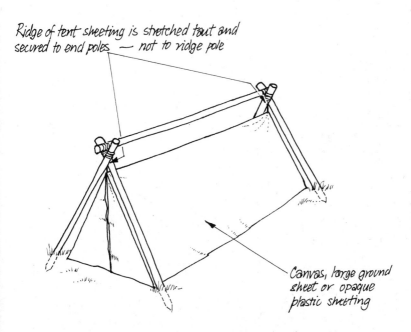

Ridge of tent sheeting is stretched taut and secured to end poles — not to ridge pole

Canvas, large ground sheet or opaque plastic sheeting

Fig 2 Erecting a tent without pegs, guy ropes or inside poles

reference: SH 6760; Ysbyty, Yr Ynys, Betws y Coed (tents and up to six caravans), SH 8153, and Carnedd, Gwerngof, Uchaf, Capel Curig (tents and a few dormobiles), SH 6759 – this last is not an official National Trust site. All are in Caernarvonshire. Campers are also welcomed by many of the National Trust's farm tenants in North Wales; apply in all cases to the farmhouse, not to the National Trust. General particulars of caravan and camping sites may, however, be obtained from the Trust's London headquarters (address above).

Youth Hostels. There are two near the eastern (Gwydyr) section of the forest park: Oaklands, half-way between Betws y Coed and Llanrwst; and Capel Curig, $\frac{1}{2}$ mile east of the village of the same name. Two others close to the western (Beddgelert) section are: Bryn Gwynant in the Gwynant valley, 4 miles from Beddgelert village; and the Snowdon Ranger Hostel on the Beddgelert to Caernarvon road (A487), facing the northern end of Beddgelert Forest.

Other accommodation. There are hotels at Betws y Coed, Beddgelert, Capel Curig and Llanrwst.

Holiday activities

Forest walks and nature trails. Snowdonia Forest Park provides ample opportunities for walking amid varying types of scenery, and affords many magnificent views. No fewer than seventeen routes are suggested in the official guide book and the locations of six way-marked trails are given in the Forestry Commission's free leaflet, *See Your Forests (Wales).* A printed guide, *Forest Walks from Betws y Coed*, is available at local shops. South of the forest park is the Coed Llyn Mair nature trail at Coedydd Maentwrog, near the B4410 in the Vale of Ffestiniog. This runs through oak woodlands and overlooks a small lake which is visited by blackheaded gulls, goldeneye, little grebes and whooper swans. The area is managed by the Nature Conservancy Council, Penrhof Road, Bangor, Caernarvonshire, from whom a leaflet may be obtained. See also *Snowdonia National Park Landscape Trails*, obtainable free of charge from the information officer of the Snowdonia National Park.

Maps. The $\frac{1}{2}$ in district map of Snowdonia covers the whole of the forest park. The more localised Ordnance Survey maps on a scale of 1:50,000 (metric equivalent of 1 in to the mile) give greater details and are more suitable for walkers and ramblers. Relevant OS sheet numbers are 115, 116, 124, 125 and 135.

Picnicking. Nine picnic sites are listed in *See Your Forests (Wales)*.

Arboretum. Three miles west of Betwys y Coed on the Holyhead road (A5). There is a picnic site nearby. Grid reference: SH 760575.

Fishing. A licence is necessary, in addition to a permit, for all fishing in Wales. Permits for fishing in the River Colwyn are obtainable from the campsite at Beddgelert. For the rivers Gwyrfai and its tributaries, apply to the Conway Fishery Board, 36 Station Road, Llanrwst, Caernarvonshire.

Climbing. The main climbing areas of Snowdonia lie mid-way between the two sections of the forest park. These are described, with the different areas and routes available for mountain walking, scrambling and climbing proper, in the *Snowdonia National Park Guide* (not the Forest Park guide).

Boating. Boats may be hired during the season on Llyn Crafnant in the Gwydyr section of the forest park. Llyn Crafnant – 'lake of garlic' – lies 3 miles due west of Llanrwst.

Places to visit

Swallow Falls. Just off the A5 between Betws y Coed and Ty Hyll Bridge (in the direction of Capel Curig) on the River Llugwy. Best seen up until late May, before the oak-tree leaves partially obscure the magnificent view.

Fairy Glen and the Conway Falls. Travelling south out of Betws y Coed, take the A5 and turn off to the right after 2 miles on to the B4406 (the Penmachno road) as far as the woollen mill (marked as an industrial site on the Wales tourist map); then bear right along the narrow lane. See the relics of the hill fort, Dinas Mawr, close to the Conway Falls, at the same time.

Conway. Take the B5106, heading north, from the market town of Llanrwst. Conway is a near-perfect example of a medieval walled fortress town. Many of the buildings have been very well preserved, but do not miss the ruined castle.

Beddgelert. The name means 'Gelert's grave', which can be seen there. According to legend, Prince Llywelyn's favourite dog, Gelert, saved a baby from a wolf, but was destroyed by his master who mistakenly believed the dog had attacked the child.

Bodnant Gardens. Two and a half miles south of Llandudno Junction on the A470. Laid out in 1875 and given to the National Trust by Lord Aberconway in 1949. A magnificent 87-acre display of broadleaves, conifers, azaleas, magnolias, rock plants and many others. The finest garden in all Wales.

Festiniog Railway. Main station and museum at Porthmadog. Runs along a causeway, then across the Glaslyn Estuary and on into the very heart of Snowdonia. Probably the oldest surviving steam-hauled and passenger-carrying narrow-gauge railway in the world.

Snowdon Mountain Railway. Climbs almost to the summit of the 3,560 ft peak of Snowdon from the village of Llanberis. Even on a hot day, it is advisable to take some warm clothing to put on at the top.

Visits may be made to woollen mills at Bryncir, Trefriw and Dinas Mawddwy and to the power stations at Ffestiniog and Harlech. For fuller details of places to visit see *North Wales*, published by the Wales Tourist Board, Llandaff, Cardiff.

Publications

Other useful publications, for which a price is charged, are:
Snowdonia Forest Park Guide, from HMSO or Forestry Commission
Snowdonia National Park Guide, from HMSO or the Information Officer, Yr Hen Ysgol, Maentwrog, Blaenau Ffestiniog, Gwynedd LL41 4HW
Wales Tourist Map, Wales Tourist Board
Guide Map to Your Forests, Forestry Commission
Also *Forestry Commission Campsites*, a free leaflet, Forestry Commission.

A list of helpful literature is available from the Information Officer of Snowdonia National Park.

The Forestry Commission's address for publications mentioned in this Snowdonia section is: Victoria House, Victoria Terrace, Aberystwyth, Dyfed SY23 2DA.

Information centres

Forestry Commission – at Gwydr Achaf, 1 mile west of Llanrwst on the B5106.
National Park – at Llanberis on the A4086.
Wales Tourist Board – at Caernarvon, near Castle Square.

Thetford Chase

Location and setting

Thetford Forest – or Thetford Chase, or Breckland, as it is severally named – extends over 80 sq miles around the towns of Thetford and Brandon on the Suffolk/Norfolk border. The forest, chiefly pine-woods, some now half a century old, is interspersed with villages and farms. The soil is mainly sand over chalk. In prehistoric times this was covered with a mixed oak forest, but Neolithic man, who established one of the greatest industrial settlements in Europe there at the time, felled most of the woodlands for use as shelter or fuel, and to make way for agriculture, of which he was the forerunner. Bronze Age man and his successors completed the work. With the protective mantle of trees removed, the area became subjected to violent sandstorms which raged, not for centuries but for millenia, inundating farmsteads and many other habitations. From the Middle Ages attempts were made to stabilise the soil by the planting of shelter belts, but it was not until the 1920s, when the Forestry Commission took over, that a really serious attempt was made to pacify this much aggrieved land. That this was successful, the 60 ft, 70 ft and 80 ft pines and firs – still reaching upwards – will testify.

About the same size in area of woodlands as Britain's largest forest park (the Glen Trool or Galloway Forest Park in Ayrshire and Kirkcudbrightshire), Thetford Chase has yet to be awarded forest park status. But, as it grows, its popularity increases year by year. Already an information centre, a woodland campsite, ten picnic sites and a number of way-marked forest walks have been set up, also an arboretum, an observation tower and a museum.

You won't do any rock climbing here for the highest point above sea level is only 183 ft. But the vast expanse of woodlands, the wildlife, the prehistoric remains, the great vault of sky and the low-rainfall continental climate make it distinctly appealing, and in some ways unique, as a forest holiday centre.

How to get there

The town of Thetford is on the A11 trunk road, 82 miles from London,

(Plate 2 overleaf) Lazing and picnicking where forest, water and heathland meet *(Forestry Commission)*

20 from Newmarket and 30 from Norwich. The main blocks of the forest lie to the north and west of the A11. Brandon is reached from the London direction by turning north off the A11 at Bacton Mills roundabout on to the A1065. Santon Downham, the village at the heart of the forest as well as its headquarters, lies 2½ miles east of Brandon on the way to Thetford.

There are two railway stations within the forest area: Brandon and Thetford, on the Liverpool Street (London)-Cambridge-Ely-Norwich line.

Details of the bus services operating in the region may be obtained from the Eastern Counties Omnibus Company Limited, Surrey Street, Norwich NOR 85B.

Plant life

Before the coming of the pine forest the plant life of the Breckland had a marked 'steppe' element about it. This still survives to some extent on the remaining heaths and on the rides and open spaces within the woods. A decided feature is the miniature size of many of the species of flora on the more impoverished, dry sandy soils. For instance, fascinating examples of dwarf viper's bugloss, forget-me-not and shepherd's purse can be found on the very poorest of the soils, fully mature and developed and no more than an inch or so high. Sandy sedge and several other coastal plants are also present. The abundance of gay summer flowers is a particular attraction, among them lady's bedstraw, wild mignonette, musk mallow, birds-foot trefoil, stone crop and black mullein. On the chalk, the yellow rock-rose, ladies fingers, purple milk vetch, horseshoe vetch, marjoram and many others may be found. It will already be seen that the flora species pattern is quite different from that of the Dean, also a southern England forest; but, on the Breckland, there are also those plants which are virtually exclusive to East Anglia – Spanish catchfly, field wormwood, spring speedwell and wild thyme.

The Breckland meres (pools and lakes), such as Langmere, Ringmere, Fowlmere and Devil's Punchbowl, have their water levels regulated by those of the chalk strata, so that they are sometimes dry in a wet season but are found to contain water in a dry season. Their flora is therefore as much, or more, dependent upon these fluctuations as upon progressional, seasonal, climatic changes. Various species of plants appear, disappear and then reappear, seemingly almost at random. This applies particularly in the case of the stoneworts and liverworts.

Wildlife

Of the mammals the most interesting are the deer – from the historian's as well as the naturalist's point of view. Deer are so dependent upon trees for their survival. Both red and roe roamed the forest in prehistoric times, but vanished when the trees were felled by early man. Now, with the coming of the pine forests, and after an interval of thousands of years, the deer are back – the red, the roe, and also the fallow, which is believed to have been introduced into Britain by the Normans.

Going to the other extreme, all three species of native shrew are present; moles are plentiful, and rabbits – after being almost wiped out by myxomatosis in 1954-5 – are again becoming numerous. Hares, bank voles, field voles and the long-tailed field mouse abound. Until recently, Thetford Forest was one of the last great refuges in England of the red squirrel. Unfortunately for them the American grey squirrel has already begun to invade this territory and, in repetition of the pattern elsewhere, the takeover may have begun. Another introduction, the South American coypu rat, is also very much in evidence. Stoats and weasels are plentiful, but otters are not common and badgers are rare.

Bats are not yet well recorded, but a number of species are known to be domiciled there. The whiskered bat has been found roosting in the prehistoric flint mines at Grime's Graves, where the bones of several other bats, including the Bechstein, have also been discovered.

As would be expected, the establishment of 80 sq miles of forest on what was formerly little more than a desert has profoundly affected the bird life. The stone curlew (old thick knees), once thought to be in peril, has adjusted himself to the changed conditions and now nests freely in forest rides and ploughed fire traces. The common curlew has also become well adapted. Populations of arboreal species such as woodpeckers, titmice, thrushes and blackbirds have all increased but, somewhat surprisingly, this has not happened with the crossbill. The missel-thrush is common and red-backed shrikes and redstarts inhabit the forest fringes. Nightjars occupy the open heaths. Species which have become more scarce include wheatear, stonechat, whinchat, redshank and ringed plover. Of the introduced game birds, the most colourful by far is the golden pheasant which, although a poor table bird – and perhaps because of it – has become widely established. The meres attract many water birds including the great crested grebe and the gadwall. Among the visitors are goosanders, Bewick's swan, both the common and the green sandpiper, greenshank and ruff.

Places to stay

Campsites. Provision for camping and caravanning is not yet good at Thetford Forest. There is, however, one very attractive Woodland Site (see page 115 for definition), with 50 pitches, among the pines of Thorpe Wood on the southern bank of the River Thet in the Norfolk section of the forest. Own sanitation is required. The site is reached from Thetford by taking the A1066 eastwards for 5 miles and then turning left on to the road signposted 'East Harling'. The site entrance is ¼ mile in on the left. Grid reference: TL 945840. There is no provision for advanced booking. See *Forestry Commission Campsites* leaflet.

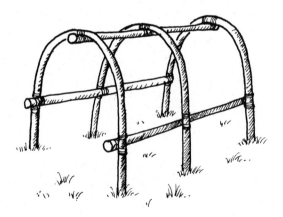

Fig 3 To make a gipsy bender you need three supple green rods (hazel or white willow are best) about 8 ft long and ½in thick, pointed at both ends, plus two or three more unpointed. Push the pointed ones firmly into the ground to form three arches and secure them by lashing the unpointed rods to them horizontally. Now you have the framework. Cover with canvas or opaque plastic sheeting and secure. A far cry from the wolf, bear and deer skins with which they were once adorned – but we have to move with the times!

Other accommodation. Hotels are the Bell and the Anchor at Thetford and the Great Eastern at Brandon. There are no youth hostels nearer than Cambridge and Norwich, both about 30 miles away. It is sometimes possible to obtain bed and breakfast in Thetford and Brandon, or in the forest villages. Certain local farmers will permit camping in their fields. Apply in all cases at the farmhouse. The Caravan Club has sites at Bacton Mills, near Mildenhall in Suffolk.

Holiday activities

Walking and nature trails. These have been very well developed in Thetford Forest. Twenty-five walks and trails, with their grid references, are listed in *See Your Forests (Southern England)*, from the Forestry Commission. Others are described in the official guide, *East Anglian Forests* (HMSO or Forestry Commission). Most of the trails are 1-3 miles in length, but for the practised walker there is a long-distance trail of 22 miles. Thetford is one of Britain's major production forests and such operations as thinning, felling and haulage of timber from the plantations to the markets are in full swing throughout most of the year. Far from detracting from the pleasure of a forest holiday, most visitors register these activities as adding to the interest and experience of the stay.

Maps. All the East Anglian forests (including Thetford Chase) are shown on the Ordnance Survey $\frac{1}{4}$ in map, sheet 14. The Ordnance Survey 1 in maps, covering Thetford Chase itself, are Nos 125, 135 and 136. A Thetford Forest map showing the locations of all the recreational facilities is available from the Forestry Commission, Brooklands Avenue, Block D, Cambridge CB2 2DY.

Arboretum. Near Lyndford Hall, once a stately home. Grid reference: TL 823943. There is a lake nearby which is on one of the forest trails.

Wildlife Observation Tower. This is situated at Santon Downham. Prior booking is necessary at the headquarters there.

Fishing. Available near Thorpe Wood campsite or information from the Forestry Commission, Santon Downham, Brandon, Suffolk.

Places to visit

Grime's Graves. Not far off the King's Lynn to Thetford road (A134). Travelling north-west from Thetford, turn left after about 6 miles at Lyndford Cross on to the B1108 towards Brandon. The entrance is about 1 mile down on the left. They are not graves at all, but Neolithic flint mines about 4,000 years old. It is the best-known site of the type in Britain. There are examples of both open-cast and underground mining. One of the shafts, about 40 ft deep, is open for visitors to descend. Galleries leading off from the bottom of the shaft were made by Stone Age miners to get at the flint. The whole area is surrounded by forest trees.

Ancient House Museum, Thetford. A fine collection of objects of prehistoric and historic local interest from the Early Stone Age through the mid and late Stone Ages, the Bronze and Iron Ages, and up to the medieval period, effectively illustrates the long story of the region. There is also a comprehensive natural history collection.

The prehistoric trackway which crosses the coast near Hunstanton on the Wash (north Norfolk coast) passes through Thetford on its way to Wessex.

Publications

The address from which to obtain Forestry Commission publications mentioned above is: Forestry Commission, Brooklands Avenue, Block D, Cambridge CB2 2DY.

The Lowther Estate

Situated at the eastern approach to the Lake District National Park, the Lowther Estate provides a great opportunity for those who wish to combine a forest, wilderness and rural holiday. Ullswater is only 5 miles away and Haweswater $5\frac{1}{2}$ miles.

This private estate, owned by Lord Lonsdale, extends to some 72,000 acres, of which 5,000 are of mixed commercial and amenity woodlands and 45,000 are common land. The estate is located around Penrith which is on the A6 and M6, partly within and partly to the east of the Lake District National Park. Lord Lonsdale, a member of the English Tourist Board, takes other people's leisure and pleasure seriously. The facilities and amenities offered to date are extremely well thought out and more developments are in progress or at the planning stage.

Caravan park

It is widely acknowledged that this particular caravan park approaches

(Plate 3) Camping beneath Great Langdale, Lake District *(National Trust)*

very near to the ideal in aesthetic planning. Opened in 1972, it stands in 48 acres of woodland on the banks of the River Lowther. The site is open from early March to late October and has permits for 326 static and touring caravans. There is also ample provision for tents. It has direct access to the A6 just south of Penrith (grid reference: NY 5226) and is only 2 miles from the M6 (exit number 40). Amenities include a children's playground and sandpit, and an off-licence and shop. Mains flush toilets, showers, water taps and disposal points are placed in vantage positions throughout the site. Dogs are permitted if kept on leash. Reservations (bank holidays only, 8 weeks in advance) for a site or a static caravan (modern and fully equipped), and all enquiries, should be made to Lowther Caravan Park, Lowther, Penrith, Cumbria.

Wildlife park

Opened in 1969 the wildlife park covers some 130 acres, about one-fifth of which is woodland. Coming from the south, leave the M6 at exit number 39, and from the north at exit number 40, and join the

A6. The entrance to the wildlife park is off this road. Grid reference: NY 5322.

In 1283 a licence was granted to the estate to make a deer park. The red deer seen in the park today are direct descendants of those introduced nearly 700 years ago. Other herds are fallow deer, Japanese and Formosan sika, and Chinese water deer. The park has also several interesting breeds of cattle, some Cheviot and Bagot wild goats, wildcats, polecats, martens, otters, foxes, badgers, water fowl and a number of other species of birds including the snowy and eagle owls, cranes and macaws. Birds and animals are placed as far as possible in their natural settings. The park has a children's play area, cafeteria and picnic areas. Dogs are not allowed into the wildlife park but may be left either in the kennels especially provided at the entrance or in the car at the carpark.

Other activities

Beacon Wood. Grid reference: NY 5231. Mainly coniferous woodland open to visitors. A large number of paths have been laid out for walking; many of these lead up to the beacon from which can be enjoyed a panoramic view of the Lakeland fells.

Millom Park. Grid reference: SD 1682. 365 acres of mixed woodland, planted subsequent to 1958 and open to the public on foot. Special paths have been laid out for walking.

Fishing. For visitors staying in the caravan park, fishing on the River Lowther, which is renowned for the sport, is available at moderate rates.

Short visits to forests (day and weekend)

Longleat Estate

Longleat, Warminster, Wiltshire, BA12 7NW. Renowned for its lions, but not so well known for its two attractive and mainly woodland scenic drives. Many of the woodland paths on this estate are open to visitors.

Goodwood Estate

Goodwood, Chichester, Sussex, PO18 0PX. Guided tours of woods (also farms and the house) are given by arrangement.

38

Brokers Wood Woodland Park

Brokers Wood, Westbury, Wiltshire. Extends to over 80 acres of mainly broadleaved forest with a further 40 acres of coniferous plantations. At the Forest Centre there is a natural history and forest museum, a lecture room (lectures held all the year round), a main exhibition hall, a library of forestry books, and a shop and tea room. Outside, a 5-acre lake provides sport in the form of coarse fishing.

There are eight basic woodland walks covering the park. Guided walks can be arranged. Pamphlets on birds and on general information are available. Natural history notes and educational aid sheets have been produced for school parties and others on payment of a nominal sum. A camping-club site and a small caravan-club site are located within the forest park. Rustic poles, stakes, pea and bean sticks, garden furniture, saplings from the woods and – in season – Christmas trees can be purchased to take back home with you. For further particulars apply to the address above.

Making your own choice

Consult the following publications:

See Your Forests (*Southern England*)
See Your Forests (*Northern England*)
See Your Forests (*Wales*)
Guide Map to Your Forests – covers England, Scotland and Wales
All the above from Forestry Commission, 231 Corstorphine Road, Edinburgh EH12 7AT.
Wales Tourist Map, from the Wales Tourist Board, Welcome House, High Street, Llandaff, Cardiff CF5 2YZ
Write to the National Trust, 42 Queen Anne's Gate, London SW1H 9AS for particulars of their forest properties.

In England and Wales few private estates, other than those detailed above, offer forest recreational or holiday facilities at the present time. None of these is listed in any publication, so a direct approach is necessary.

When planning your forest holiday, use a selection of the above publications, and other information gained, in conjunction with those given under the headings appropriate to your needs in Part C, Chapter 2 (Selection of Accommodation) and Part B (Forest Holiday Activities).

2 Scotland

Water, woodlands and wilderness – these are the main ingredients of a forest holiday in Scotland: spruce and pine soaring from the shores of lochs to the mid-slopes of mountains, heather and crag above. And always the quiet contrast of the sheltered glen with its oaks, birches and other broadleaved trees.

Argyll Forest Park
Location and setting

The Argyll Forest Park, situated among the beautiful hills and lochs of the Cowal peninsula, is the oldest one in Britain, having been established in 1935. It lies between Loch Long and Loch Fyne, with part of its north-eastern boundary fringing on Loch Lomond. Its 66,000 acres are made up of six forest blocks: Ardgarten, Glenbranter, Loch Eck, Glenifinart, Benmore and Loch Goil. From north to south it covers 18 miles. There are four main peaks within the park: Ben Ime, 3,318ft; Ben Narmain, 3,036ft; Ben Arther (or the Cobbler), 2,891ft and A'Chrois, 2,785ft. There are several others and also a number of other lochs.

How to get there

The terrain is so well broken up by peaks and lochs that ways of getting into the forest park are limited, although the roads which do serve it are good and easily motorable. Travelling north from Glasgow the A82 runs along the western bank of Loch Lomond to Tarbet. Turn left at Tarbet on to the A83, passing through Arrochar 2 miles on. One mile beyond Arrochar, at the head of Loch Long, is the northern boundary of the forest park. For travellers from the north of Scotland, the A82 can be joined at Crianlarich, 16 miles north of Arrochar. There is another way in – to the park's southern boundary – via the ferry from Gourock across the Firth of Clyde to Dunoon. The forest park boundary is about 3 miles on from there.

The nearest railway station is at Tarbet (Arrochar and Tarbet railway station). There is also a long-distance bus service from Glasgow to Campbeltown. Local bus services operate within the forest park.

Plant life

The movements of the Great Ice Age moulded and fashioned this land from which the forests of Argyll rise, influencing the type and variety of vegetation growing upon it. Another factor determining the species of flora is that no part of the forest park is more than 4 miles from the sea and the sea lochs (those which are open to the sea). These, bearing their salt water, stretch far inland. Then there is the tempering influence of the Gulf Stream. All these things combine to ensure that the plant life of the forest park is at least as rich as any to be found anywhere in the United Kingdom.

Marine vegetation, such as the red, brown and green seaweeds, are washed up along the shores of Loch Goil and Loch Long. A striking feature of many of the valley slopes is the exceptionally rich covering of lichens, mosses, liverworts and ferns, probably equalled only by Cornwall, the most south-westerly county of England.

Apart from the timber crop trees of spruce, pine and larch, the river valleys are heavily stocked with natural ash, birch, alder and willow, with oak, elm, holly and rowan coming in on the better-drained ground a little above.

The ground flora includes water lobelia, water millfoil, horsetail, quillwort and stonewort; and, again on the drier land, wild hyacinth, primrose, anemone and violet. On the higher slopes and heaths there is blaeberry (bilberry), bracken, ling heather, fine-leaved and cross-leaved heaths, sedges and rushes with cotton grass, and sphagnum moss in the wetter places. A number of alpine plants exist above the 2,000ft contour.

Wildlife

Red deer, wild cat, polecat, otter, red fox, stoat, weasel, hedgehog and grey squirrel are some of the animals you may chance to see. Among the birds are the golden eagle, peregrine falcon, kestrel, sparrow hawk, buzzard, heron, raven, kingfisher, swan, goose, duck, black grouse, capercaillie and ptarmigan. The goldcrest is resident throughout the year. Together with many others I have omitted, they make a very impressive list. Reptiles and amphibia are also well represented.

Fig 4 Cut this tent peg from natural roundwood – oak, ash, chestnut or beech are best but any strong wood will do

Places to stay

Camping. There is a large and particularly attractive Class A (see page 115 for definition) Forestry Commission caravan and camping ground situated on a promontory which juts out into the salt waters of Loch Long. It is on the side of the A83 about 2 miles west of Arrochar. Advance bookings for 7 days or more, at least 14 days in advance, should be made to The Warden, Forestry Commission Camp, Ardgarten, Argyllshire. The campsite has 280 pitches and takes both tents and touring caravans.

Three other camping sites within the boundaries of the forest park are listed in *Scotland for Touring Caravans* (from the Scottish Tourist Board, 23 Ravelston Terrace, Edinburgh EH4 3EU): two on Loch Eck and one at Lochgoilhead. Only one has accommodation for tenters. There is also a Camping Club site at Ardgarten, not far from the Forestry Commission camp.

Youth hostels. There is one youth hostel at Ardgarten and another at Strone Point.

Other accommodation. Hotels in and around the park are at Tarbet, Arrochar – a very good centre for the west coast of Scotland – at Lochgoilhead, Carrick, St Catherine's, Creggans near Strachur, Whistlefield and Coylet beside Loch Eck, Cot House near Ardberg, Kilmun, Strone, Blairmore and Ardentinny.

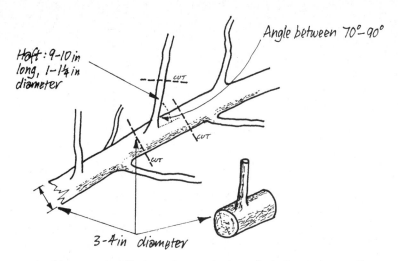

Haft: 9–10 in long, 1–1¼ in diameter

Angle between 70°–90°

cut

cut

cut

3–4 in diameter

Fig 5 This tent-peg mallet is cut from natural wood – holly, elm or yew for preference. Heavier mauls for driving in latrine and other stakes can be made from the stouter end of the same trunk or from a thicker trunk

Holiday pursuits

Forest walks and nature trails. There are several forest walks in the Benmore section of the park, beginning at grid reference point NS 145855 on the A815, Strachur to Dunoon road 1½ miles south of Loch Eck. Another is on the same road near Glenbranter village: grid reference NS 123976, 15 miles north of Dunoon; with a further one on a by-road 1 mile south-east of Strachur: grid reference NN 105006. However, in a land of such breathtaking scenic beauty it is not difficult, and sometimes preferable, to plan one's own walks and hill climbs with the aid of map and compass.

Maps. Ordnance Survey 1 in maps covering the park are numbers 53, 58 and 59. Part of it is also included on the *Loch Lomond and Trossachs Tourist Map* (1 in to the mile).

Picnicking. There are two picnic sites within the park: one at the northern end of Loch Goil, grid reference NS 202062; and the other on the eastern shore of Loch Eck, grid reference NS 142925.

Boating. Boats may be hired at Arrochar and at the Ardgarten campsite.

Bathing. There is good salt-water bathing at the Ardgarten camping ground beside Loch Long, and also at several other salt and fresh watersides on the various lochs throughout the park.

Fishing. For fishing in River Finart and sea-angling on Loch Long, apply to the Forestry Commission, 21 India street, Glasgow G2 4PL.

Rock climbing. The four main peaks within the Argyll Forest Park, together with their subsidiaries, attract a large number of climbers every year, particularly as they are situated among some of the finest scenery of the West Highlands.

Places to visit

Arboretum. Kilmun Arboretum and forest plots are on the Dunoon-Strone-Ardentinny road (A880), grid reference NS 165824.

Botanical Gardens. The Younger Botanical Gardens – a landscaped garden of great variety and beauty near Benmore House, a large mansion in the Scottish baronial style, formerly the home of the Youngers. The extensive gardens are managed in association with the Royal Botanical Gardens, Edinburgh, and contain one of the world's finest collections of rhododendrons, as well as the arboretum. Grid reference: NS 144855.

Puck's Glen. Close to Benmore House. A very popular beauty spot from which a path winds its way up to a fine lookout point where a memorial rest-shelter commemorates Sir Isaac Bayley-Balfour, one of the great Scottish botanists.

Inverary Castle. The home of the dukes of Argyll and the head-quarters of the Campbell clan since the 15th century. The present castle was built in the 18th century in the French *château* style and greatly admired by Sir Walter Scott. Fine furniture, plate and tapestries. Extensive gardens. A remarkable and impressive setting. Only 16 miles from the forest park, it is well worth a visit.

Publications

Argyll Forest Park Guide, HMSO or Forestry Commission
Guide Map to Your Forests, Forestry Commission
Scotland Touring Map, Scottish Tourist Board, 23 Ravelston Terrace, Edinburgh EH4 3EU
Scotland 550 Things to See, Scottish Tourist Board
Forestry Commission Campsites and *See Your Forests* (*Scotland*) are available free of charge from the Forestry Commission

The Forestry Commission's address for publications mentioned in this section is: 21 India Street, Glasgow G2 4PL.

Information centres

There are Scottish Tourist Board information centres at Gourock (pier head) and Dunoon – that is, on either side of the Firth of Clyde on the ferry route leading to the southern entrance to the forest park; at Tarbet (Stuckgowan) just outside the northern entrance, and at Ardgarten (near the campsite) within the park itself.

Glen More Forest Park

Location and setting

Situated on the north-western slopes of the Cairngorm mountain range in Inverness-shire, with crags and moulded summits all around, and with Loch Morlich (1,000ft above sea level) at its heart, the Glen More Forest Park is Britain's only truly all-season holiday forest. Here, one can ramble, hill walk, rock climb, sail and swim in spring, summer and autumn, and ski and skate in winter and early spring.

The forest park has 3,400 acres of pine and spruce woods, plus a further 9,000 acres of grass- and heather-clad moorland. Cairngorm Mountain (4,084ft), from which the range takes its name, lies just within the southern boundary of the park. Loch Morlich is a beautiful expanse of clear, fresh water, nowhere more than 25ft deep; it has long lengths of sandy beaches, fringed and shaded here and there by gaunt old Caledonian pines, and absolutely ideal for both adult and infant holidaymaker.

How to get there

Coming from the south, take the main road from Perth to Inverness (A9) and turn right on to the A951 over the new Spey Bridge just before Aviemore. This new road leads directly to the campsite, the youth hostel and the forester's office 7 miles further on.

Train travellers should write to British Rail for the *Golden Rail* brochure. Nearest railway station is Aviemore. Express trains from Edinburgh, Glasgow and Inverness stop there. Then, by bus, taxi or hired car from Aviemore to the Glen More campsite.

(Plate 4 overleaf) Loch Morlich Beach, Glen More Forest Park, Cairngorms *(L.S. Paterson)*

Plant life

The forest park, with its neighbouring forest of Rothiemurchus, forms part of the Cairngorm Nature Reserve of the Nature Conservancy Council and offers a very wide range of plant subjects for study. The Scots pine, the dominant woodland tree in the region, is almost certainly a survivor from just after the last Ice Age. Juniper and birch – also native trees – occasionally occur among the pines and, with them, blaeberry (bilberry), ling heather, cowberry, serrate wintergreen and chickweed wintergreen, also the edible morel mushroom. Open growing, on the slopes of the mountains and in the glens, you will find pine, birch, rowan and juniper with such ground flora as bell heather, petty whin, twayblade, cloudberry, crowberry, bear berry and, more rarely, cat's ear. Aquatic plants, such as water lobelia and the lesser spearwort, thrive around the loch, and, in the wet, boggy areas and along burnsides, cross-leaved heath, bog asphodel, spotted orchis, butterwort and sundew. On the higher ground, up to 3,000 ft, are stunted shrubs of the azalea family, cushions of moss campion, the small rush, alpine lady's mantle, bog vaccinium (relative of the bilberry and cowberry) and dwarf cornel. Above 3,000 ft, where the vegetation is sparse, the twigs of the dwarf willow rise only an inch or so above

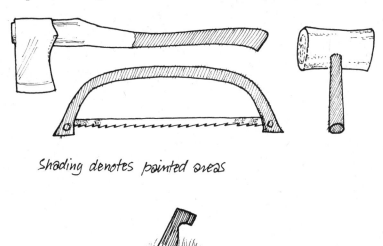

Shading denotes painted areas

Fig 6 Paint camping tools red or white to stand out against greens and browns of the undergrowth. Paint tent pegs to avoid toe stubbing

the ground, with cowberry and moss campion still persisting, and globe flower in the more sheltered aspects of the corries. Also found are various species of saxifrage and many mosses and liverworts belonging to high altitudes.

Wildlife

A great feature of the forest park is the free-ranging herd of reindeer which has been introduced in recent years. Red deer, in large numbers, also roam the hills, while roe deer inhabit the plantations and thickets. Another feature is the mountain hare, whose fur changes to white in winter as a camouflage against the background of snow. Also represented are the wild cat, fox, otter and badger.

Bird rarities include the crested tit, the snow bunting and, some-

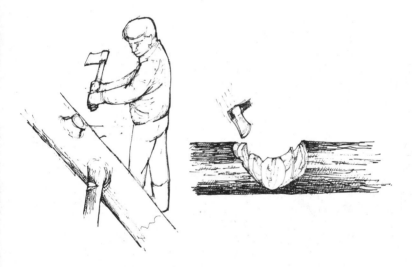

Fig 7 Axing the safe way – (A) When trimming a fallen tree trunk, keep the log between yourself and the axe for protection. Trim as close to the trunk as possible (except see Fig 14). Always make sure that your hands and the haft of the axe are dry and free from mud or grease. Even then, it could still slip out of your hands – so keep other campers well out of range
(B) For crosscutting with an axe, be sure to start with a wide enough V – about the diameter of the log. If you don't, you will only have to widen it later, taking many more strokes and using a lot more energy. Stand on firm, clean ground with feet wide apart, and as the axe has to be lifted or swung above the head, ensure that there are no obstructions such as low boughs of nearby standing trees

times on the very summits, the dotterel. Another bird of the heights – a game bird – is the ptarmigan. Lower down come the capercaillie and the red grouse (chiefly on the open moors), and the black grouse (mainly in the coverts). The crossbill is very active in the pinewoods. Among other species, including the raven and the crow, one must not forget the golden eagle which may, if you are patient or fortunate, be seen soaring above even the highest summits.

What was once Britain's most stirring wilderness has now become one of the foremost inland holiday centres in the kingdom. But this is really 'big country', the land of the Cairngorms, and because there is ample space, and thanks to thoughtful and careful planning, the world of nature and the realm of man-made pleasure exist successfully hand in hand.

Where to stay

Camping and caravanning. The Glen More campsite (220 pitches for caravans and tents) is a Class A (see page 115 for definition) site and lies directly under the Cairngorm ski areas on the eastern shore of Loch Morlich: grid reference NH 974095. It is open all the year round, for tourists in the spring and summer, and for skiers in the winter. A large recreation room is open to campers. In addition to the usual Grade A facilities there are two shops offering a full range of supplies and provisions, one with a sub-post office and a public telephone kiosk. There is also a small teashop. For information regarding campsites, the address is: Head Forester, Forestry Commission, Glen More, Aviemore, Inverness-shire.

Youth Hostels. The Loch Morlich Youth Hostel, also at the Glen More address, is on the same stretch of open ground as the campsite. For other youth hostels in the region, contact the Scottish Youth Hostels Association, 7 Bruntsfield Crescent, Edinburgh.

Other accommodation. Seven miles away at Aviemore (on the A9) there is a very wide range of accommodation. There is a caravan park which admits tenters and has toilets, showers and a shop. Hotels in Aviemore are the Strathspey, the Badenoch and the Post House. There is also a chalets motel. For further details and free leaflets, write to the Aviemore Centre, Aviemore, Inverness-shire, or to the individual establishment at the same address.

Holiday pursuits

Walking. There are three forest walks within the park. Apply at the forest office for map and printed guides. In addition, there are numerous hill paths all around which afford splendid views.

Maps. Ordnance Survey 1 in sheet No 38, Grantown and Cairngorm, covers nine-tenths of the forest park. Sheet No 37, Kingussie, covers most of the neighbouring Rothiemurchus Estate, where there are some very attractive woodland walks. Bartholomew's ½ in sheet No 51, the Grampians, includes the whole of the Cairngorm Forest Park, the Rothiemurchus Estate and Aviemore, but is not as detailed.

Riding. Nearest riding stables are at Aviemore and Newtonmore.

Bathing. On Loch Morlich. Safest and best bathing is at the east end, near the campsite, where there is a dry, sandy shore. Non-swimmers should beware and children should be accompanied by an adult, as there are deep hollows in the bed of the loch.

Boating. Available on Loch Morlich. Apply forest office. Also available on the neighbouring estate of Rothiemurcus. For the latter apply at Aviemore post office. There is a sailing school at Glen More Lodge, near the forest park campsite, which is run by the Scottish Sports Council, 4 Queensferry Street, Edinburgh EH2 4PB, and another at Aviemore – write to Aviemore Centre, Aviemore, Inverness-shire.

Fishing. Coarse fishing is available on Loch Morlich. Apply forest office. Game and coarse fishing is also available on the Rothiemurchus Estate bordering on the forest park. Apply Aviemore post office.

Skating. Open-air skating may be enjoyed on Loch Morlich in winter when the ice is thick enough. Enquiries as to whether conditions are safe can be made at the Information Room near the campsite or the Scottish Council for Physical Recreation at Glen More Lodge, also near the campsite. There is also an indoor ice-rink at Aviemore.

Ski-ing. Although in an exceptional year skiers can be seen on the slopes of the Cairngorms from mid-November to early summer, the normal season is from mid-December until the end of April or – to play very safe – say, January to April inclusive. The earlier months of

(Plate 5 overleaf) Pony Trekking in the grounds at the Aviemore Centre, Inverness-shire *(Aviemore Centre)*

January and February are the slackest time on the ski slopes, but arctic conditions may well be encountered for short or longer spells during this period.

The road to the Cairngorm ski area (known as the Ski Road) begins at the Glen More campsite. There are two car parks at the ski area, which is also served by bus. The ski area has four chair lifts and six ski tows. There are snack bars and restaurants at various levels, with the famous Ptarmigan Observation Restaurant – the highest in Britain – at the top of the White Lady Chairlift, 3,600ft above sea level. From here, there are absolutely magnificent views over the Strathspey and beyond.

Sports shops catering for skiers are in all the main towns and villages. Equipment and clothing can be hired; apply for free information leaflet to The Secretary, Cairngorm Sports Development Ltd, 26 Church Street, Inverness. The Scottish Council for Physical Recreation at Glen More Lodge holds residential ski-ing courses, stages talks and film shows, and organises social amenities and functions, as well as hiring out skis, sticks and boots. All enquiries concerning these matters should be made to the Council's offices at 4 Queensferry Street, Edinburgh EH2 4PB – not to Glen More Lodge. There are also several ski schools in the towns and villages round about. Write to the Scottish Tourist Board, 23 Ravelston Terrace, Edinburgh EH4 3EU, for their booklet, *Winter Sports in Scotland*.

Ski-bobbing and toboganning are also popular on the slopes. For beginners, and for all skiers during unsuitable conditions, there is an artificial ski run at Aviemore.

Aviemore Holiday Centre. On the A90 at Aviemore. The centre is open all the year round. In addition to the holiday accommodation detailed above, its activities are very wide ranging and include golf, tennis, table tennis, squash, swimming (indoor heated and outdoor pools), skating (ice rink), curling, trampolining, crazy golf, dancing and folk singing. There is a sauna bath, a solarium (sun bathing throughout the year) and a children's playground, also conference rooms, an exhibition hall and a craft centre. Write to Aviemore Centre, Aviemore, Inverness-shire for further particulars.

Rock climbing. Walks and climbs are organised, and instructions on hill walking, rock climbing, mountain safety and field studies are given by fully qualified instructors, on specified weeks (full board) throughout the summer at Glen More Lodge, the Scottish Centre for Outdoor Training close to the forest park campsite. All enquiries should be addressed to the Scottish Sports Council, 4 Queensferry Street, Edinburgh EH2 4PB. Included in the fee are the social amenities, talks and film shows in progress at the time, as well as transport between Aviemore railway station and Glen More Lodge.

Places to visit

Loch-an-Eileen Visitor Centre. On the B970, $2\frac{1}{2}$ miles south of Aviemore. A lochside cottage exhibition depicting the development of the region from the last Ice Age up to the present time. A nature trail also starts here. The loch itself is well worth a visit in its own right for its charming setting amidst ancient pinewoods. The ruined castle on the islet was founded about the 15th century and has been held at various times by the Mackintoshes, the Gordons and – from 1567 – the Grants.

Highland Wildlife Park. Just off the A9, 5 miles south-west of Aviemore. No entry after 6pm. This 250-acre drive-through wildlife park is famous for showing, in their natural surroundings, such creatures as wolves and bears which once lived in the Highlands, together with many still present, including deer and wildcat. There are 26 species of mammals and 24 species of birds.

Carrbridge Visitor Centre. At Carrbridge on the A9, 8 miles north of Aviemore. Winner of the British Tourist Authority's main award for the most outstanding development of 1970. The first of its kind in Europe, this 'landmark' visitor centre dramatically unrolls 10,000 years of Highland history in the triple-screen, audio-visual theatre. In addition, there are static exhibitions of the history of Strathspey, a bookshop, a craftshop and a restaurant, also a board-walk nature trail through the pinewoods to a viewpoint of the Cairngorm Mountains.

Am Fasgadh (*The Shelter*). At Kingussie on the A9, 12 miles south-west of Aviemore. A Highland folk museum with a comprehensive collection of Highland dress, tartans, old craft relics and farm implements. Nearby are a period furnished cottage, a clack mill and other items of interest.

Ruthven Barracks. On the B970, across the Spey River from Kingussie. This is where Prince Charles' Highlanders regrouped after the disastrous battle of Culloden in 1746. Extensive ruins.

Publications

Glen More Forest Park Guide (priced), from HMSO or Forestry Commission.

Forestry Commission Campsites (free), Forestry Commission.

See Your Forests (Scotland) (free), Forestry Commission.

The Forestry Commission's address for publications in this section is: 21 Church Street, Inverness IV1 1EL.

Information centres

Forestry Commission Information Room – at the Glen More campsite.

Scottish Tourist Board Information Centre – at the Central Car Park, Aviemore.

Atholl Estate

The Duke of Atholl's estate at Blair Atholl on the A9, some 35 miles north of Perth, 7 miles north-west of Pitlochry and 3 miles from Killiecrankie, is virtually in the centre of Scotland. Blair Atholl railway station is on the main line from Glasgow, Edinburgh and Perth to Inverness. The setting of this estate in the forest-clad Highlands is the realisation of a painter's or photographer's dream and offers magnificent opportunities for all kinds of forest holidays.

Where to stay

The Blair Castle Caravan Site. Map reference: Ordnance Survey sheet 49/872655. Situated in the castle grounds between the main drive and the River Tilt, this is a modern, 30-acre site, opened in 1971 and licensed to accept 315 caravans/tents. There are also 12 large residential (6-berth) caravans for letting during the holiday season, positioned in a secluded spot backing on to the river. These are fully equipped except for linen and towels. All enquiries (with stamped addressed envelope) to The Warden, Blair Castle Caravan Site, Blair Atholl, Pitlochry, Perthshire PH18 5SR.

Holiday cottages. The estate has four holiday cottages for letting. Minimum let is one week, with stays of two, three or four weeks attracting a reduction of 5, 7 and 10 per cent respectively. Two of the cottages carry optional fishing permits for trout, and one has permits for salmon and trout. For particulars apply: The Factor, Atholl

Estates Office, Blair Atholl, Pitlochry, Perthshire PH18 5TH.

Other accommodation. Hotels in Blair Atholl are the Atholl Arms and the Tilt. There are also good hotels at Killiecrankie and Pitlochry.

Holiday activities and interests

Blair Castle. About ten minutes' walk from the campsite. The local bus from Blair Atholl stops outside the castle gates. Open Easter weekend; Sundays and Mondays in April, and daily from the first Sunday in May until the second Sunday in October. The stronghold of the earls and dukes of Atholl for centuries, the castle has many historical connections, the oldest part dating back to 1270. Edward III stayed there in 1336 and Mary Queen of Scots attended a hunt in the Atholl Forest in 1564 – when the bag included five wolves! The castle was occupied for eight years by the Cromwellians. The 32 rooms open to the public depict Scottish life from the 16th to the present century. There is a restaurant at the castle.

Forest walks and nature trails. Two short trails, partly through woodlands, operate in conjunction with the campsite. A further 10-mile trail in Glen Tilt, covering a much higher proportion of woodland, is currently being prepared. There is a highly scenic riverside walk and nature trail at the Linn of Tummel owned by the National Trust for Scotland; approach from the car park just over the bridge leading off the A9 to Rannoch. There are four forest walks (2-6 miles long) in the large state forests of Tummel in the locality. For these, take the A9 from Blair Atholl, travelling south to Killiecrankie (3 miles), and turn right on to the B8019, then continue for a further 3 miles. At this point (grid reference: NN 863598) there is also a Forestry Commission Information Centre. Enquire there concerning other trails, particularly the Loch Faskally trail from Pitlochry.

Loch Tummel Visitor Centre and Queen's View. On the B8019 at the Forestry Commission Information Centre. The Loch Tummel Visitor Centre, opened in 1972, tells the story of the Tummel Valley, its forestry, archaeology, history and industry. Near the Centre is Queen's View – visited by Queen Victoria in 1866 – a splendid viewpoint along Loch Tummel to the peak of Schiehallion (3,547ft). The four forest walks begin at Queen's View. There is also a picnic spot. The Loch Tummel area is a must for visitors to the centre of Scotland.

Pitlochry Dam, Fish Ladder and Power Station. Part of the Tummel

Valley hydro-electric development. Migrating salmon can be observed through underwater windows at the fish ladder. Hydro-electric power exhibition. Car park. Lochside walks.

Pitlochry Festival Theatre. In the words of the National Trust for Scotland, 'Stay six days and see six plays.' First-class repertory performances from April to September. Celebrity concerts on Sundays.

Riding. The two hotels at Blair Atholl – the Atholl Arms and the Tilt – organise pony-trekking excursions and may, from time to time, be in a position to let out mounts for riding.

Fishing. Permits for fishing are carried by one or two holiday cottages on the estate (see above).

Lilliardsedge Park

This is part of an estate of the Marquess of Lothian and, although it cannot yet claim, in itself, to provide forest holidays, it does have interesting woodland connections and would make a useful port of call in a mixed touring holiday.

Where to stay

Camping. There is a well-laid-out caravan and camping site on the side of the main road from Jedburgh to Edinburgh (the A68) 5 miles north-west of Jedburgh. It has a restaurant, snack bar and tavern, also a shop, play area and garden centre. The site office has a large stock of tourist literature, and staff are pleased to assist visitors in planning itineries. Riding and fishing can also be arranged. Address: The Warden, Lilliardsedge Park, Jedburgh, Roxburghshire.

Furnished houses. There are four furnished houses to let on a holiday basis – two with fishing on beats of the River Teviot and two without. Write for further particulars to: The Factor, Lothian Estates Office, Jedburgh, Roxburghshire.

Other accommodation. There are hotels in Jedburgh, Selkirk and Hawick.

Activities and interests

Woodland walk and arboretum. A woodland walk should have been set up by the time this book is in print. Enquire at the campsite office. The Monteviot Arboretum on the estate was begun in the middle of the last century and carries a wide range of both broadleaved and coniferous specimens. Although not open to the general public, access will be granted to anyone interested on application to the estate office.

Border Forest Park. Jedburgh is less than 20 miles north of the Border Forest Park, which is the second largest in Britain and extends into Roxburghshire, Dumfries-shire, Cumbria and Northumbria. Take the B6357 leading off the A68 to the right a couple of miles south of Jedburgh. The B6357 runs through the north-western edge of the Border Forest Park.

Glentress Forest. Two miles east of Peebles on the A72. Grid reference: NT 284396. The forest has three picnic places and three forest walks. Take the A68 from Lilliardsedge Park, travelling north, and fork left on to the A72 some 7 miles on. On the way, around Melrose, you will pass through and near other forest areas, where there is also a car park and picnic site.

Other things to see and do. The region is renowned for its historic abbeys: at Jedburgh (5 miles from the campsite), Melrose (8 miles), Kelso (12 miles) and Dryburgh (5 miles). Famous houses include Traquair House and Mellerstain House.

The locality is well served with golf courses, swimming pools, tennis courts and bowling greens. The campsite office will provide full information.

Conifers Leisure Park

This is an especially attractive and useful centre in Galloway for a combined forest, rural and coastal holiday. Its great advantage is its soft, mild climate which extends the holiday season over nearly eight months of the year and brings an early spring. This is also an artist's and photographer's paradise.

How to get there

Travelling north, take the A75 from Gretna Green through Annan, Dumfries and Castle Douglas. About one mile before Newton Stewart turn right on to the A712. The entrance to the Conifers

(Plate 6 overleaf) Woodland chalets, Conifer Leisure Park, Wigtownshire, *(Conifer Leisure Park)*

Leisure Park is the first turning on the left about 200 yards on from the junction, along the private road signposted 'Kirroughtree Hotel'. The Conifer Park lies just behind the hotel and is open throughout the year. Grid reference: NX 422662. The Park is essentially for the motorist and makes an ideal retreat.

Accommodation

This consists of 24 chalets situated in an attractive natural setting of a 25-acre mature pinewood. The chalets, imported from Finland, are furnished and equipped to a very high standard of comfort. Only the linen is not supplied. There is a small children's play area. The Kirroughtree Hotel, adjacent, is fully licensed. All enquiries and bookings to the Conifers Leisure Park, Newton Stewart, Wigtown-shire.

Leisure facilities

Horse riding is provided for next to the park. Golf, sailing, climbing, shooting and fishing (river, loch and sea) are all within easy reach. Full particulars from the park office.

Places of interest

Galloway Forest Park. Immediately to the north of the Conifers Leisure Park lies the largest forest park in Britain – now Galloway but formerly named Glen Trool. Extending to over 130,000 acres, with the lovely Loch Trool as its central feature, and embracing other lochs as well as many fells and crags, the park is set in some of Scotland's most glorious scenery, where red and roe deer roam, also herds of wild goats. Forest walks and picnic sites are numerous. The forest park, together with the surrounding countryside and coast, comprises a veritable haven for gulls, swans, geese, ducks, whaups, grouse and buzzards.

Galloway Deer Museum. Ten miles from the Leisure Park. On the A712 (the road which leads from the A75 to the Conifers Leisure Park) beside Clatteringshaws Loch. Grid reference: NX 550760. There is a Forestry Commission Information Centre nearby.

Wild Goat Enclosure. Six miles from the Leisure Park on the A712 7 miles north-east of Newton Stewart. Grid reference: NX 495723.

Arboretum. On a by-road off the A75 at grid reference NX 453635,

(Plate 7) A forest cabin above the shores of Loch Lubnaig, Strathyre Forest, Perthshire *(Forestry Commission)*

just north of Palnure. Palnure is 3 miles south-east of Newton Stewart.

Newton Stewart. With a population of about 2,000, it is the only town of any size in the area. It is a pleasant market town with five hotels – including the Kirroughtree – and inns.

Other places to see. While you are in this corner of Britain do not forget to visit Burns' Cottage at Alloway (south of Ayr). Also, not 10 miles from this, Culzean Castle, home of the Kennedy clan; 556 acres of the grounds became Scotland's first country park in 1970. There are some fine woodland walks.

Strathyre Forest

Strathyre Forest is the home of the Forestry Commission's pioneer scheme, launched in 1973, and provides log-cabin accommodation for visitors. This type of forest holiday, entirely new to Britain, has proved immensely popular and no doubt the idea will spread to other woodland areas.

How to get there

Coming from the south, make for Stirling, then take the A84, heading north-west through Callander, the hamlet of Kilmahog and the densely wooded Pass of Leny. As you emerge from the Pass, look out for the sign: 'Forestry Commission – Strathyre Forest Cabins' and turn left off the A84 at this point. Travellers from the north should pick up the A84 at Lochearnhead, drive through Strathyre village and all the way down past Loch Lubnaig. At its end, look for the above Forestry Commission sign and turn off to the right. In either case, after turning off the A84, cross the river bridge and immediately turn left, then follow the former railway line by Loch Lubnaig to the cabins.

Stirling is the nearest railway station and motorail terminus. There is a bus service from Stirling via Callander.

Accommodation

The cabins are constructed of larch logs, with natural materials – wood, wool, cotton – used internally wherever possible. Each cabin is fully equipped with shower, cooker and fridge, and consists of kitchen/diner, living-room/lounge, verandah and two bedrooms, to accommodate five persons. The lounge window in each case affords magnificent views of Strathyre Forest and Loch Lubnaig. Bed linen

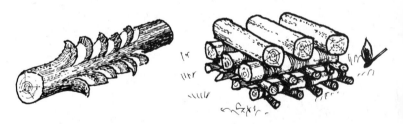

Fig 8 To start a camp fire in wet weather use birch bark from fallen or dead standing trees, pine cones, or make prayer sticks by cutting partly through the wood and prising slivers apart with a sharp knife. Softwood (conifer) is better than hardwood. Alternatively, use dry paper, dry grass or dry bracken. As soon as your fire has caught alight, begin placing pre-gathered sticks and then logs on the fire criss-cross fashion, small ones first, gradually increasing in size as flames take hold. Don't be in too much of a hurry or you will smother it. Conifer, birch, ash, oak, beech are all good fuelwoods but almost anything will burn once a fire is blazing. Always ask permission before lighting a camp-fire. Always put a fire out thoroughly before leaving a site or going to bed. Hearths are provided at some camp and picnic sites

and towels are not supplied, as it is claimed that most visitors prefer to bring their own. These can, however, be hired, provided the housekeeper is given prior notice. The cabins are connected to mains services and fitted with electric fires and water heaters. Electric supply is by coin in the slot. Pets are welcome but should be kept under proper control. Local traders will deliver provisions, which can be ordered in advance. Callander, $3\frac{1}{2}$ miles away, is a small town with good shopping facilities, banks, doctor, dentist, chemist, garages and taxi service.

The cabins – in 1975 there were only seventeen but more are planned – are booked up well in advance, in some cases two years ahead; so, if this kind of holiday appeals to you, it would be wise to get your name on the list as early as possible. Write for booking forms and literature to: Forestry Commission, West Scotland Conservancy, 20 Renfrew Street, Glasgow G2 3BG.

Holiday activities

Walking and nature-trailing. The position of the cabins, situated between forest and loch, provides ample opportunities for the casual walker. For the more serious exercise of hill walking there is Ben Ledi which rises above the forest behind the cabins to a height of 2,873ft. In addition, two way-marked trails have been laid down in Strathyre Forest: one starting beside the A84 just south of Strathyre village (grid reference: NN 562168); the other adjoining Callander town

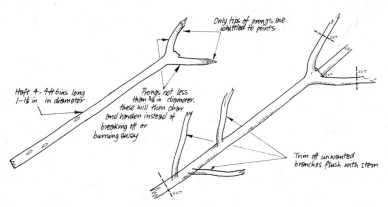

Fig 9 A long-handled fork can be made for tending a campfire. Ash, oak, sweet chestnut, holly, sycamore are the best woods to use

$\frac{1}{4}$ mile north of the central road junction (grid reference: NN 863081).

Picnicking. There are numerous natural picnicking spots around the shores of Loch Lubnaig and, within the forest, two 'furnished' picnicking sites – one at the beginning of the way-marked trail south of Strathyre village and the other at Leny Pass south of Loch Lubnaig (grid reference: NN 594089).

Fishing. Permits, giving access to a variety of Perthshire waters, can be obtained from local hotels and shops. More detailed particulars are available from the information centres.

Canoeing. There is canoeing within the forest on Loch Venachar.

Sailing. On Loch Venachar and Loch Earn.

Riding. Enquire at the Forest Information Centre.

Water ski-ing. On Loch Earn.

Golf, tennis, bowling. Course, courts and green at Callander.

Steamer trips. From the eastern end of Loch Katrine, on the *Sir Walter Scott*; fine views include Ben Lomond. On Loch Lomond: from Balloch Pier, north of Dumbarton, the *Maid of the Loch* sails the length of the loch with opportunities to disembark.

Information centres

The Forest Information Centre is in Strathyre village. There is also the Callander and District Tourist Information Bureau at Callander.

Places to visit

The Queen Elizabeth Forest Park. Some 46,000 acres in extent, stretching from the Trossachs to the eastern shores of Loch Lomond, and touching on Loch Katrine and Loch Achray, its northern boundary is only 8 miles from the Strathyre cabin site. Enquiries concerning its wide range of amenities and activities should be made at the David Marshall Lodge, $\frac{1}{2}$ mile north of Aberfoyle on the A821 (grid reference: NN 520017). Loch Ard and Loch Chon are within the forest park, as also are the mountains of Ben Lomond (3,192ft), Ben Venue (2,393ft) and the Menteith Hills. The locality is the setting for Sir Walter Scott's famous novel, *Rob Roy*, and for his poem, *The Lady of the Lake*.

Making your own choice

Consult the following publications:

See Your Forests (Scotland)

(Plate 8) Orienteers racing home through alder woods on the shores of Loch Lomond. Queen Elizabeth Forest Park, mid-Scotland *(H.L. Edlin)*

Guide Map to Your Forests
Also see *Catalogue of Publications* for list of forest park guides.
All the above from the Forestry Commission, 231 Corstorphine Road, Edinburgh EH12 7AT.
Scotland Touring Map, from the Scottish Tourist Board, 23 Ravelston Terrace, Edinburgh EH4 3EU.
Write to the National Trust for Scotland, 5 Charlotte Square, Edinburgh EH2 4DU for particulars of their woodlands.

For private estates offering forest recreational facilities and holidays, other than those given above, write to Scottish Recreational Land Association, Haig House, 23 Drumsheugh Gardens, Edinburgh EH3 7RN.

Use the above publications and other information gained in conjunction with those given under the headings appropriate to your needs in Part C, Chapter 2 (Selection of Accommodation) and Part B (Forest Holiday Activities).

3 Ireland

Northern Ireland being part of the United Kingdom, visitors from Great Britain can enter and travel without restriction. No passport or green card is required, but some travellers find it convenient to carry a passport at the present time.

For entry into Southern Ireland (Eire), no passport is necessary, but visitors with cars must take with them a valid driving licence, log book and green insurance card; there are also restrictions on the import of certain items into Eire and duty is charged on others. However, generous duty-free allowances meet most reasonable needs. Full particulars are contained in *Customs Guide for Tourists* from the Irish Tourist Board, Box 273, 63–67 Upper Stephen Street, Dublin 8 or from any of their information centres. There are no restrictions on dogs and cats but, as birds of the parrot family are subject to quarantine, your budgie will have to stay at home. British bank notes and currency may be freely used in all parts of Ireland.

There are thirty-five air routes and nine sea routes between Britain and Ireland. All sea routes have drive-on drive-off services. Travel agents will provide full information and book your passage for you. Alternatively, write for particulars to the Irish Tourist Board in Dublin, or to the Northern Ireland Tourist Board, River House, 48 High Street, Belfast BT1 2DS.

With a total population of half that of London, Ireland offers

Fig 10 Many coniferous and some broadleaved trees grow with curved stems and they are in great demand by the rustic trade. A carefully selected one will make a good yoke for carrying buckets of water or bundles of firewood. Some fashioning with a billhook or paring knife may be needed. Exact dimensions cannot be given as this is the sort of thing that has to be tailor-made, but, for an adult, the overall length is about 3ft, the diameter of the thickest part approximately 3in, tapering to $1\frac{1}{4}$–$1\frac{1}{2}$in at the ends

carefree motoring; and, because there are so few built-up areas, caravanning is an ideal form of holiday. Caravanning, of course, combines very well with a forest holiday.

All holiday forests in Ireland – both north and south – are managed by the respective forestry authorities. In the private forestry sectors, the matter is under active review and it is possible that a limited number of estates may have forest holiday facilities in the near future. In Ireland, as in Great Britain, the forest-holiday industry is still in a stage of development.

Forest parks and other recreational forests in Ireland are considerably smaller than those in Britain. Ideal as ports of call, or for short stays, they do not lend themselves so readily as full-length-holiday resorts. The emphasis in this section therefore is on the touring aspects of Ireland's forest areas.

Northern Ireland (Ulster)

The Northern Ireland forestry authority (The Forestry Division of the Department of Agriculture, Dundonald House, Upper Newtonards Road, Belfast BT4 3SB), unlike the other two forestry authorities in the British Isles, imposes an admission charge for entry into each of its five forest parks and certain other woodland areas with recreational developments. This entry charge should not be confused with the car park, campsite and arboretum admission charges which are common, with a few exceptions here and there, to all forestry authorities and private estates offering forest-recreational facilities. However, the Northern Ireland entry charge is not more than one would normally expect to pay for access to, say, the house and grounds of a National Trust property. Wherever an entry charge is imposed, there is a Forest Ranger in post who assists in the control and maintenance of the recreation area, and is available to answer queries and assist visitors. Season permits for cars and mini-buses can be obtained which give access for one year to all forests bearing an entry charge. These are of interest to residents in Ireland and can be purchased either from the Forest Ranger on site or from the Forestry Division of the Department of Agriculture.

Only about 10 per cent of the 150,000 acres of the Forestry Division's land in Northern Ireland has been developed for public recreation. The remainder is managed primarily for the growing of timber and

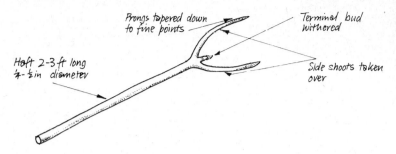

Prongs tapered down to fine points

Terminal bud withered

Haft 2-3 ft long ¼-½ in diameter

Side shoots taken over

Fig 11   A simple toasting fork

retains the impression of natural wilderness. Most timber forests, however, are open to the public on foot. (See *Outdoors in Ulster*, HMSO).

Forest parks and leisure areas

The five forest parks are at Gosford Castle, County Armagh; Castlewellan and Tollymore, County Down; and Drum Manor and Gortin Glen, County Tyrone. There is a priced leaflet available for each park, as well as leaflets about nature trails, or tree trails, which can be obtained on site. The parks at Gosford Castle, Castlewellan and Tollymore have Forest Caravan Sites or Forest Touring Caravan Sites (see page 114 for definitions), and Gortin Glen has a camp (tents only) site. Each forest park has a car park and picnic site.

Gosford Castle Forest Park, which takes its name from the enormous mock-Norman building close by, is situated just north of Markethill, on the road from Armagh to Newry (A28). It has fine gardens and an arboretum.

Castlewellan Forest Park and Tollymore Forest Park are within 3 miles of each other. Tollymore is less than 2 miles from the coastal town and resort of Newcastle and in the northern foothills of the Mountains of Mourne – the most compact area of beauty in the whole of the British Isles, according to H. V. Morton. Tollymore Forest Park is situated on the southern side of the B180. Turn left off the A50 2 miles out of Newcastle – but not before you have seen the California red-woods in Donald Park.

(Plate 9 opposite) Strolling in a coniferous forest in summer, Tollymore Forest Park, Northern Ireland *(Northern Ireland Tourist Board)*

Castlewellan Forest Park lies just west of the town of that name on the northern side of the A50, in equally enchanting country. Here there is lakeland fishing – and you should be happy with the result for, according to the Irish, even a beginner can catch better fish in Ireland than an expert can in England.

Both forest parks have arboreta and gardens, also adjoining riding stables where ponies may be hired.

Gortin Glen is a beautiful forest park amid the hills of North Tyrone, with mature broadleaved and coniferous trees, a quiet stream and secluded picnic areas. There is also an attractive scenic drive, a wildlife enclosure, and a barbecue site. The B48, running south from Gortin, passes through the forest park.

Drum Manor Forest Park, some 18 miles to the east, and only about 11 miles from the western shore of the famous Loch Neagh, is smaller than the others and in lowland countryside. Its butterfly garden is unique and well worth a visit from nature lovers and from professional and amateur naturalists alike. There you can learn methods which will enable you to attract butterflies to your own garden. Drum Manor Forest Park lies at the left-hand side of the A505, 4 miles out of Cookstown, travelling west towards Omagh.

Other leisure forests. There are thirty-four other forests with recreational areas: six in County Antrim, three in County Armagh, five in County Down, five in County Fermanagh, eight in County Londonderry and seven in County Tyrone. All have car parks, picnic places and planned walks. Precise locations of all these on a map, together with much other information, are contained in *Outdoors in Ulster's Forests*, from HMSO.

Scenic drives. In addition to the one at Gortin Glen Forest Park, there are scenic drives at Ballycastle, County Antrim; Loch Navar Forest, County Fermanagh, and at Rostrevor, County Down.

Maps. The excellent $\frac{1}{4}$ in to the mile relief map of Northern Ireland, published by the Northern Ireland Tourist Board, River House, 48 High Street, Belfast BT1 2DS, gives a considerable amount of detail for its scale. It depicts such useful facilities and amenities as bird sanctuaries, scenic routes, view points, youth hostels, caravan and camping sites and, of course, information bureaux. On the back of the map are featured seven circular tours, taking in beauty spots, places of antiquity and other tourist attractions. Most of the routes pass through or near many of the holiday forests. With this map, and the one in *Outdoors in Ulster's Forests*, you will be equipped to plan your own tailor-made combined forest and general touring holiday.

With only 26 cars for every mile of road, compared with 64 in Britain; with no more than half an hour's drive to the coast in any direction, and with a string of recreational forests a lot nearer than that, such a holiday in Northern Ireland has all the ingredients of an experience you will always remember.

Southern Ireland (Eire)

Eire has over 300 forest areas open to the public, including six forest parks, with two more in the making. Just over half these woodland areas have some holiday or recreational activity or development. All twenty-six counties in Eire are represented. No entry charge is made, but a car park fee is payable at the forest parks (for which a season ticket may be obtained). Certain of the forest areas are somewhat remote – not actually a disadvantage in this day and age – but difficulties have sometimes been experienced in locating them. To make matters easier, forests have been given the names by which they are known locally, so when in doubt, just ask. In any case, many of the forest picnic areas have now been signposted in advance along public roads.

Planning your own tour

The best way to enjoy a forest holiday in Eire – and this applies to both residents and visitors – is to provide yourself with a copy of *The Open Forest*, published by the Forest and Wildlife Service, 22 Upper Merrion Street, Dublin 2, plus a good general map of the country, and work out your own route.

The Open Forest lists, by counties, all the 300 forest areas, with brief descriptions of their amenities and facilities. According to the tour you finally decide upon, guide books of forest parks, nature trail brochures, etc, can then be purchased direct from the Forest and Wildlife Service or at the forests themselves, and local maps obtained to fill in the details.

Maps. A very useful general map is that published by the Irish Tourist Board, Box 273, 63–67 Upper Stephen Street, Dublin 8. It includes Northern Ireland as well, and shows all the youth hostels

Fig 12 Spindlewood makes clean and useful meat hooks and skewers but strip off bark down to bare wood before use

(both An Óige and Yhani) throughout the two countries, many of which are in localities where the most attractive holiday forests are to be found. There is no upper age limit for staying at youth hostels, by the way. The map also gives air and sea routes to and from Ireland, tour routes (roads) and information on currency, customs and weather, as well as addresses of the Irish Tourist Board offices in Britain.

Local maps come in three scales: $\frac{1}{4}$ in, $\frac{1}{2}$ in and 1 in to the mile; I would recommend the largest of these – the 1 in. If you have the Irish Tourist Board map (12 miles to the inch), you won't need either of the other two.

Other printed aids. It would be useful to have by you *Caravan and Camping Parks*; *Town and Country Homes, Farmhouses, in Ireland*, and *Hotels and Guest Houses in Ireland*, all from the Irish Tourist Board. A guide book which will greatly assist you in planning the actual route is the Irish Tourist Board's *Motoring in Ireland*. It describes six circular tours of Eire, including the grand scenic tour of Ireland which also takes in Ulster. These tours are especially designed to cover pretty well all the tourist highlights in Eire; so that, by using one or more of them as the basis for a general and forest holiday tour, you can get the best out of both worlds. You may well wish to modify the tour in places, depart from the route here and there, and then return to it again. But it will serve as a useful aid, and there is more fun and satisfaction to be gained from a holiday you have had a personal hand in shaping than in one you have merely 'reached down from the shelf'. Here are two of these 'official' tours to help you plan your route.

Irish Tourist Board Tour No 2

Main ports of call: Dublin – Navan – Dundalk – Drogheda – Skerries – Howth – Bray – Glencree – Glendalough – Arklow – Wexford –

New Ross – Kilkenny – Carlow – Athy – Kildare – Dublin.

Within easy range of this route there are no fewer than 68 forest areas open to the public, 38 of which have one or more types of recreational facility or sporting activity. Two are forest parks and one has an adventure centre. County Wicklow tops the list with Avondale Forest Park, the Tiglin Adventure Centre, 16 forests with recreational facilities and 16 with woodland walks and views only.

Avondale Forest Park (530 acres) lies 1 mile south of Rathdrum and has planned walks, nature trails and picnic sites. Avondale House, which was the home of Charles Stewart Parnell, is open to the public Monday to Friday (pm) from May until September. A printed guide is available, which includes the forest trails, the history of the estate and an account of wildlife.

Tiglin Adventure Centre is in the well-known Devil's Glen Forest, 2 miles west of Ashford on the road to Glendalough. The forest has a waterfall and there is a car park, a nature trail and a picnic area, as well as forest walks. The adventure centre, established in 1972, comes under the AFAS (Association for Adventure Sport). The first in the country, it is open full-time – ie not only at weekends – and holds courses varying in length from one day to one week. These are for young people and adults, youth leaders and teachers, school parties and other organisations. The standards of the courses are set according to proficiency, and cover such subjects as orienteering, canoeing, mountaineering, rock climbing and field studies. By taking one or more – or combining two – of the AFAS courses, your forest-holiday experiences would undoubtedly be deepened and enriched. Full particulars from: The AFAS Booking Secretary, 1 Rock Hill, Blackrock, County Dublin.

John F. Kennedy Forest Park, County Wexford, is 8 miles from New Ross on the L159. There is a car park, arboretum and forest garden, picnic area, shop/restaurant, viewing point and planned walks. A brochure is available on site. The county has nine other forest areas open to the public. One of these – Dunamore Forest – has attractive riverside and forest walks, viewing point and a picnic area. Stop at the car park at Dunamore Bridge, 3 miles from Enniscorthy.

Slieve Foyle Forest, County Louth, 2 miles from Carlingford on the T62 towards Omeath, has a scenic drive to the car park overlooking Carlingford Lough and a picnic area.

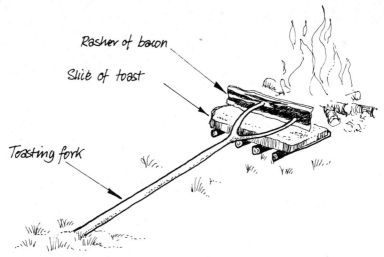

Rasher of bacon

Slice of toast

Toasting fork

Fig 13 Cook bacon gipsy fashion for a succulent breakfast. Point haft end of toasting fork shown in Fig 11 and toast a slice of bread. Place toast on sticks near campfire and fix rasher of bacon to prongs of toasting fork. Insert pointed haft of toasting fork in ground so that bacon is face-on to the fire and is held directly above the toast. Fat will drip down and soak into the toast. Turn bacon as required. Incidentally, kippers cooked gipsy fashion are equally delicious. Open out a newspaper, wrap the kipper in it, then throw – yes, throw – it on the fire. When the newspaper has burnt through and is black all over, rescue the fish from the flames with your toasting fork. Inside the charred remains of the newspaper will be a beautifully cooked kipper. Once you've sampled it you'll never want to do them any other way!

Fishing can be had at Lough Bracken in County Meath, 1 mile south-west of Drumconrath off the L24. There is also a car park, a picnic area and woodland walks.

Climbing. For climbers and hill walkers, access to Three Rock and Two Rock Mountains, County Dublin, is from Three Rock Mountain Forest, 5 miles south of Rathfarnham. Turn south on signposted cul-de-sac off the L93. There is a car park, forest walks and panoramic views.

Irish Tourist Board Tour No 3

Main ports of call: Cork – Kinsale – Skibbereen – Bantry – Glengariff – Kenmare – Waterville – Cahirciveen – Glenbeigh – Killarney – Tralee – Ballyheigue – Foynes – Limerick – Tipparary – Cashel – Cahir – Lismore – Youghal – Cork. There is a short detour to Blarney Castle from Cork.

Fig 14 Clothes become messy at or near ground level and certain wild animals – notably foxes – have cultivated a remarkable taste for processed foods. For a clothes stand or vertical larder, find a well branched, standing dead tree and cut the branches to within 6in–1ft of the trunk. Alternatively, find a felled, or naturally fallen, tree – permission will need to be obtained first – and treat it in the same manner, then bury the butt in the ground. Food should always be well wrapped and suspended from the tips of the severed branches in string, cloth or plastic bags to defeat birds, insects and climbing mammals. A net thrown over the whole is a sound additional precaution

Within and around this route – which includes the mountain ranges of Kerry, the Golden Vale of Tipperary, and the beauty that is Killarney – two forest parks and 120 other forest areas (67 with recreational developments) await you; many of them in the most luxuriant scenery imaginable. County Cork has the most with 55 forests, Gougane Barra Forest Park among them. County Waterford has 33, County Tipperary 16, County Kerry 12; and, although County Limerick has but 6, Currahchase Forest Park is one of them.

Gougane (or Gaugan) Barra Forest Park (850 acres) lies 2 miles off the T64 at the Pass of Keimaneigh. It provides an original form of forest recreation with its motor trail. This is particularly valuable for the elderly or disabled who are denied the pleasure of following the nature trails and walks on foot. Notes are given in the forest guide, so that these can be read out by a passenger in the car as the trail proceeds. There are also several wooded walks and a fully documented nature trail, as well as a car park and picnic area. History, geology, wildlife and traditions are all engagingly – one might almost say, poetically – described in the printed guide of this beautiful forest park. I was much taken by two lines of J. J. Callanan's poem, *Gaugin*, for instance, which so aptly describe this great coum in storm: 'And the waters come down 'mid the thunder's deep rattle, Like clans from the hills at the voice of the battle'.

Cahermurphy Forest, near Flagmont, has its car park right on the shores of Lough Graney. There are swimming facilities nearby, also walks in the woods.

Castlefreke Forest, off the L42 , 6 miles from Clonakilty, runs down to the sea coast and has a car park, picnic areas and forest walks.

Dunboy Forest, 2 miles west of Castletownbere on the L61, has sea-shore and forest walks.

Farran Forest is 3 miles south-east of Coachford on the Coachford to Farran road. Here there are forest and lakeside walks, also a car park, picnic area and scenic views.

Marloge Forest, off the Cobh to East Ferry road (turn right just before East Ferry) has viewing points overlooking Cork Harbour, as well as car park, picnic area and forest walks.

Dromore Forest, on the Kenmare to Sneen road (T66) 6 miles west of Kenmare, has a viewing point overlooking Kenmare Bay; also picnic area and seashore walk.

Coolfree/Glenanaar Forest lies 10 miles north-east of Mallow on the T38. Hill climbs and forest walks can be enjoyed here in the Canon Sheehan country.

Currahchase Forest Park, on the Limerick to Askearton road (T68), is of recent creation. There is a car park and picnic area, and gardens, an arboretum and woodland walks are planned. The ruins of Currahchase House, home of Aubrey de Vere, are nearby. Enquire at Kilcornan for directions.

Greenwood Forest, 3 miles west of Kilfinnane or 6 miles south of Kilmallock, off the Kilmallock to Kildorrey road (L36). More hill climbs, again in the Canon Sheenan country, at Fanningstown. The forest also has a car park, picnic area and woodland walks.

Bohernagore Forest, at the Vee Hairpin Bend on the L34, has a viewing point overlooking the Knockmealdown Mountains, and forest walks.

Glengarra Forest, 8 miles south-west of Cahir on the T6 (main Dublin to Cork road), has some unusual species of trees and shrubs; also riverside and forest walks, nature trail, car park and picnic area. Trail leaflet is available on site.

Knockballinery Forest lies about mid-way between Clogheen and Newcastle on the road which links with the L28 south of Clogheen. There is a wooded scenic drive and riverside walks.

Marl Bog Forest, on the Dundrum to Tipperary road, about 1 mile from Dundrum, gives access to a game sanctuary. There is also a car park, picnic area and woodland walks.

Forest walks. For spring holidaymakers there are some fine rhododendron paths – and forest walks – at Coolfin/Glenhouse Forest ½ mile beyond the Roman Catholic Church in Portlaw; also at Macallopglen Forest ½ mile north of the Ballyduff to Fermoy road and 2 miles west of Ballyduff village.

More woodland and riverside walks are at Dromana Forest on the Villierstown to Cappoquin road; at Glenarey/Russelstown Forest 2 miles south of Clonmel, off the T27; and at Glenshellane Forest, 2 miles north of Cappoquin (turn right at the Grotto off the Mount Melleray road).

Forest holiday plans

The forests mentioned above are only a small selection of those to be found on Irish Tourist Board Tours Nos 2 and 3. Such is the variety of scenery in Eire – woodland, rural, mountain, loughland and seaside – and such the diversity of natural and manmade features, that any tour you devise is bound to be a memorable one. The picture is the same all over southern Ireland.

It would be perfectly feasible – as the mean radius of the six official circular tours is no more than 30 miles or so – to select a base somewhere near the centre of any one of them and to cover a high proportion of the holiday forests on or near the route by means of day visits. (See Part C, Chapter 2 for holiday accommodation in Eire).

It is equally possible, with the aid of maps, forest holiday literature and accommodation guides, to plan your own forest holiday tour independently of any of the prescribed ones.

PART B

Forest Holiday Activities

Introduction

Activity holidays in the forest are divided here into two kinds, the physical and the cultural. Sources are given from which further information can be obtained, including particulars of day and residential courses.

It is perfectly possible – indeed, usual – to combine a number of activities in one holiday. This section will help you to sort out your preferences in advance, and to equip and inform yourself accordingly. It also enables you to track down those forests – other than the ones already covered in Part A – which cater for your particular needs.

On the other hand, you need not be active at all in order to enjoy a forest holiday. In fact, it is popular with many just because it provides an unique opportunity to relax and benefit from 'the therapy of the green leaf'.

1 Active Pursuits

Walking

There are hundreds of way-marked forest walks throughout the British Isles. A high proportion are instructive – ie, they are nature trails. Additionally, a growing number of forests are opening up to the public their road and ride systems. In total, they represent many thousands of walking miles.

A plan of the road and ride systems open to the public is obtainable at certain forests. Failing this, a 6in Ordnance Survey map sheet of the locality, bought at stationers, shows the roads and rides of the longer-established forests. Otherwise a 1 in map of the district and a pocket compass are recommended.

A word of warning! Many forests are in high mountainous country where rapid weather changes can be hazardous. Temperatures plummet quickly. When walking in these areas, take a companion with you, and set out well equipped with extra clothing, food and hot drink. Remember, one mile of hill country equals three elsewhere.

Forest walks are listed and/or described in the following publications:

Scotland for Hillwalking, Scottish Tourist Board, 23 Ravelston Terrace, Edinburgh EH4 3EU.

Activity Holidays in England 2, English Tourist Board, 4 Grosvenor Gardens, London SW1W 0DU.

Nature Trails in England, English Tourist Board.

The Open Forest, Forest and Wildlife Service, 22 Upper Merrion Street, Dublin 2.

See Your Forests in four parts: (Northern England, Southern England, Scotland or Wales) Forestry Commission, 231 Corstorphine Road, Edinburgh EH12 7AT.

Nature Walks, National Trust, 42 Queen Anne's Gate, London SW1H 9AS.

For Northern Ireland, obtain trail leaflets at individual forests.

Many private estates also provide trails and attractive forest walks. Enquiries to estate office.

The Sports Council, 70 Brompton Road, London SW3 1EX, runs fell-walking courses throughout the summer, in consultation with the Ramblers' Association – on map and compass techniques, route selection and timing, choice of equipment and load carrying.

Information about any aspect of walking is obtainable from the Ramblers' Association, 1–4 Crawford Mews, London W1H 1PT.

Driving

Forest driving takes two forms, along public roads in wooded country or on private roads through the trees. The private roads are especially selected for their scenic beauty and known as scenic drives, or scenic forest drives. A toll charge is often imposed for road upkeep and amenity improvement. Most drives have parking bays at points along the way where the vista is particularly fine. Except for scenic drives and access to car parks and picnic areas the car is excluded.

In much forest country, petrol stations are few and far between, so keep a close watch on your petrol gauge.

A stationary vehicle, with its windows closed and its occupants remaining still behind the glass, tends to be ignored by wildlife. Woodland animals, which might otherwise go unobserved, can often be seen in this way, especially early or late in the season when broad-leaved and larch trees are bare.

Forest drives are given in the following publications:

Abbeys, Moors, Forest and Coast, Yorkshire Tourist Board, 312 Tadcaster Road, York YO2 2HF.

See Your Forests in four parts: (Northern England, Southern England, Scotland and Wales), Forestry Commission, 231 Corstorphine Road, Edinburgh EH12 7AT.

The Open Forest, Forest and Wildlife Service, 22 Upper Merrion Street, Dublin 2. Also, their *Gaugan Barra Forest Park Guide* has a very interesting motor trail.

Forests, Country Parks and Nature Reserves, Northern Ireland Tourist Board, 48 High Street, Belfast BT1 2DS.

Obviously, a fairly large tract of well-established forest is needed for the setting up of a scenic drive, so the majority are found in state forests. However, certain of the larger private estates now have plans in hand to provide these. The Longleat Estate, near Warminster in Wiltshire, already has two scenic forest drives.

(*Plate 10*) A scenic drive through Allerston Forest, North Yorkshire (*W.R. Mitchell*)

Picnicking

Forest picnic areas in the British Isles number many hundreds, with new ones coming into being all the time. They are so well distributed that hardly any city or town is more than half an hour's drive away from at least one.

They are invariably sited in the most attractive part of the woods, often alongside a lake or stream, and are usually equipped with serviceable and durable tables and benches. If litter bins are not provided, rubbish should be taken away and not left around to mar the pleasure of others. When accompanied by the elderly or disabled, choose a picnic area with a car park nearby or, preferably, where parking is permitted on the picnic site.

The Countryside Club, 109 Upper Woodcote Road, Caversham Heights, Reading, Berkshire, runs a scheme of picnic areas and woodland walks for its members. The woodlands, to which only members have access, are numerous and cover from 25 to 1,000 acres each.

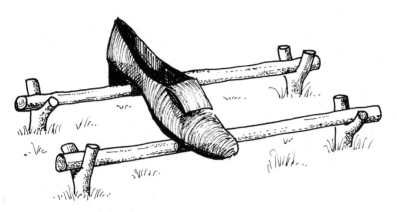

Fig 15   An alternative to the illustrated boot and shoe rack is to tie the laces together and hang the boots or shoes on your clothes rack (Fig 14) or over the branches of a nearby tree

Picnic areas are included in the following publications:
The Open Forest, Forest and Wildlife Service, 22 Upper Merrion Street, Dublin 2.
See Your Forests in four parts: (Northern England, Southern England, Scotland and Wales), Forestry Commission, 231 Corstorphine Road, Edinburgh EH12 7AT.
Forests, Country Parks and Nature Reserves, Northern Ireland Tourist Board, 48 High Street, Belfast BT1 2DS.
Many forest picnic areas are shown on the tourist maps issued by the tourist boards, and on *Guide Map to Your Forests*, published by the Forestry Commission. They are also given in literature issued by the various national park authorities of England and Wales.

The Countryside Commission, John Dower House, Crescent Place, Cheltenham, Gloucestershire GL50 3RA, publishes a list of recommended (mainly local authority) picnic sites, with a map covering England and Wales. Only a small percentage of these are in woodlands and not all have yet been set up.

Rock Climbing

Main regions are the Lake District, Peak District, North Yorkshire and Dartmoor in England; Snowdonia in Wales; the Cairngorms in Scotland, and the Wicklow Mountains in Ireland. All these, and others, are within or near forest parks or other holiday forests.

Rock climbing, which is only for the physically fit, comprises a series of skills and techniques between fell-walking and mountaineering. Potentially dangerous, it should never be attempted unless under the guidance of a qualified instructor, or until competence has been attained. Never rock climb alone.

A list of climbing clubs and information on rock climbing can be obtained from the British Mountaineering Council, Room 314, 26 Park Crescent, London WIN 4EE. A very good book on climbing is *Where to Climb in the British Isles* by Edward C. Pyatt (Faber & Faber).

Courses on rock climbing are held at:

Tiglin Adventure Centre (in Devil's Glen Forest), Ashford, County Wicklow, Eire.

Plas y Brenin National Mountaineering Centre (in Snowdonia Forest Park), Capel Curig, Betws y Coed, North Wales.

Scottish Centre of Outdoor Training (in Glen More Forest Park), Glenmore Lodge, Aviemore, Inverness-shire.

Storrs Hall (nr Thornthwaite Forest), Windermere, Cumbria.

There are a number of other rock-climbing course centres throughout the British Isles; although not in or near holiday forests, these could, for those living within range, serve as useful pre-holiday training centres. Write to the British Mountaineering Council (address above) for information.

The Peak National Park publishes an instructive little booklet: *The Story of Climbing in the Peak National Park*. Write to Peak Park Planning Board, The National Park Office, Baslow Road, Bakewell, Derbyshire DE4 IAE.

Riding

Almost all holiday forests have riding stables within or close to their boundaries. While most stables cater for family parties, some concentrate either on teenagers or adults, or on novices or more experienced riders. Preliminary enquiries are therefore advisable. The forest holiday centre of your choice will give you addresses of riding establishments in the locality; while national park, tourist board and forest park information centres also maintain lists.

Unlike pony-trekking holidays, which are seasonal and for set periods, riding can be enjoyed all the year round, and mounts hired by the hour, half day or day. It is a sport that can be fitted in with other forest holiday pursuits.

Whatever gear is worn, a hard hat and strong, low-heeled footwear are advisable, and waterproof clothing may prove useful. Moss Brothers hire out riding clothes and equipment from stock at their London shop in Bedford Street, Covent Garden, and also, if given advance notice, at their provincial branches.

There is a good distribution of riding schools – many in or near holiday forests – for those wishing to learn to ride or improve their horsemanship; again, some of these specialise. Lists of riding schools are published by The British Horse Society, National Equestrian Centre, Stoneleigh, Kenilworth, Warwickshire CV8 2LR; Ponies of Britain, Brookside Farm, Ascot, Berkshire SL5 7LU; and the Association of British Riding Schools, Chesham House, 56 Green End Road, Sawtry, Cambridgeshire.

Riding schools and stables are listed in the following publications:
Forests, Country Parks and Nature Reserves, Northern Ireland Tourist Board, 48 High Street, Belfast BT1 2DS.
Pony Trekking and Riding, Wales Tourist Board, High Street, Llandaff, Cardiff.
Pony Trekking and Riding in Scotland, Scottish Tourist Board, 23 Ravelston Terrace, Edinburgh EH4 3EU.

The tourist maps of the Scottish Tourist Board and Wales Tourist Board also give locations of riding stables. Some riding establishments provide accommodation for visitors.

Activity Holidays in England 3, English Tourist Board, 4 Grosvenor Gardens, London SW1W 0DU, gives useful hints and information to riders.

Ski-ing

The best ski slopes are in the Cairngorms, in the Glen More Forest Park, in Scotland, where snowfalls are fairly predictable. Ski-ing is also possible in Snowdonia, in and near the Snowdonia Forest Park, North Wales; and in parts of northern England whenever the snow pattern is right.

In the Cairngorm area, there is a Forestry Commission campsite, a youth hostel and the famous Aviemore Centre, with hotels, motels and chalets, and many après-ski attractions. Skis and ski clothes can be hired at Aviemore, and tuition is given both on snow and on plastic slopes. (See pages 51 and 54 for further information.)

The official ski-ing season in Britain is from December to May and it would be taking an undue risk to book outside these times.

For grass ski-ing – a comparatively new all-the-year-round sport – there are a number of centres, useful for pre-holiday instruction and practice. Courses on grass and plastic are organised by the Ski Club of Great Britain, 118 Eaton Square, London SW1W 9AF, and a list of artificial ski slopes can be obtained from the National Ski Federation of Great Britain at the same address.

For snow ski-ing and artificial ski slopes in Wales write to Plas y Brenin National Mountaineering Centre, Capel Curig, Betws y Coed, North Wales, or to the National Ski Federation of Great Britain.

In England, the White Hall Centre, Long Hill, Buxton, Derbyshire, includes snow ski-ing in its activities when conditions are right. Allenheads Lodge, Allenheads, Dovespool, Northumberland, also has ski-ing facilities. The North York Moors National Park, County Hall, Northallerton DL7 8AD, has a list of ski-slopes within the park.

See the following publications:

Scottish Sports Holidays, Scottish Tourist Board and Scottish Sports Council from the STB's address at 23 Ravelston Terrace, Edinburgh EH4 3EU.

Winter Sports in Scotland, as above.

Activity Holidays in England 2, English Tourist Board, Dept AH, 4 Grosvenor Gardens, London SW1W ODU.

Cairngorm Ski Area (and other leaflets) from the Aviemore Centre, Inverness-shire.

Forestry Commission Campsites, Forestry Commission, 231 Corstorphine Road, Edinburgh EH12 7AT.

Swimming

For those who participate in water sports of any kind the ability to swim is an essential safeguard against loss of life. A sailing boat may capsize, a canoe spring a leak. . . . Swimming, of course, is a sport in its own right and the lochs, lakes, pools and rivers in the holiday forests of the British Isles are among the most exhilarating anywhere. It needs to be borne in mind, however, that unless a certain standard of competence has been reached, and without knowledge of local conditions, many of them can prove hazardous. Always enquire at the local forest information centre or office before taking the plunge. The bed of a lake or loch may have deep hollows, and the rate of flow of mountain rivers and streams can accelerate dramatically after a heavy rainstorm.

For swimming tuition, the Amateur Swimming Association, Derby Square, Loughborough, Leicestershire, should be able to put you in touch with the nearest swimming pool where professional instruction is given. This association holds residential summer schools at its Loughborough headquarters, giving first-class tuition on all types of swimming under every condition, with lectures in the evenings.

More and more hotels are equipped with swimming pools, as is shown in accommodation brochures from the various tourist boards and other sources. See *Hotels with Swimming Pools and Golf Courses*, Scottish Tourist Board, 23 Ravelston Terrace, Edinburgh EH4 3EU.

For swimming facilities in Ireland see *The Open Forest*, Forest and Wildlife Service, 22 Upper Merrion Street, Dublin 2. For other holiday forests, find out, when making general enquiries, whether swimming facilities exist.

Boating

There are many lakes, lochs, inlets and rivers in or near the forest parks or other holiday forests of the British Isles where sailing and canoeing can be enjoyed. A number of these are shown on the tourist maps issued by the Scottish Tourist Board and the Wales Tourist Board. Anyone unable to swim at least 25 yards, preferably 50 yards, should not go sailing or canoeing. Canoes are, however, very stable and in normal conditions are difficult to capsize – particularly by children, because of their lower centres of gravity – so that canoeing is a lot safer than it looks.

Much useful information on sailing and canoeing – the purchase or hire costs of vessels, type of craft suitable, additional equipment required – can be found in *Activity Holidays in England 1*, from the

(Plate 11 overleaf) Canoeing and sailing on Lake Gerionydd, Snowdonia Forest Park *(Forestry Commission)*

English Tourist Board, Dept AH, 4 Grosvenor Gardens, London SW1W ODU.

Scottish Sports Holidays, from the Scottish Tourist Board, 23 Ravelston Terrace, Edinburgh EH4 3EU, describes canoe camping and the advantages of sailing and canoeing in Scotland.

The Wales Tourist Board, Welcome House, High Street, Llandaff, Cardiff, issues a leaflet, *Sailing and Water Sports*, with a map on which is marked the full range of water sports and their locations.

Canoeing instruction is given at the Tiglin Adventure Centre, Ashford, County Wicklow, Eire, in the beautiful Devil's Glen Forest. There are a number of lovely rivers and lakes nearby.

Sailing and canoeing courses are arranged in Britain by the Sports Council, 70 Brompton Road, London SW3 1EX. See their booklet, *Taking Part in Sport*. Prospective pupils must be able to swim 50 yards before acceptance by either organisation.

The British Canoe Union, 26–29 Park Crescent, London W1N 4DT will forward a list of their publications on request.

The Royal Yachting Association, 5 Buckingham Gate, London SW1E 6JT, publishes a list of its recognised teaching establishments.

Fishing

Game fishing (salmon and trout) and coarse fishing (other edible freshwater fish) are both available in the holiday forests of the British Isles. Trout fishing is far less expensive than salmon fishing, and coarse fishing the cheapest of the three. Preferably, choose a forest holiday resort which has its own stretch of water and where permits are issued. The law in respect of fishing varies from country to country and from region to region, as do closed and open seasons for the different types of fish. Enquiries must therefore be made locally about fishing rights and regulations, and also whether a licence as well as a permit is required.

Scotland

The Scottish Tourist Board, 23 Ravelston Terrace, Edinburgh EH4 3EU, publishes an excellent 124-page guide to salmon and trout fishing (certain other fish, too): *Scotland for Fishing*. It lists literally hundreds of fishing grounds with addresses, types of fish to be caught and permit prices by day, week and season. Against each entry is a map key by which it can be located on one of the eleven pages of maps at the back of the guide. For coarse fishing see the Scottish Tourist Board's leaflet, *Scotland for Coarse Fishing*. By using these guides in conjunction with the *Scotland Touring Map* (from the Scottish Tourist Board) or *Guide Map to Your Forests* (from the Forestry Commission, 231 Corstorphine Road, Edinburgh EH12 7AT), it becomes a simple matter to link up likely fishing grounds with the holiday forest of your choice.

Wales

Angling, from the Wales Tourist Board, Welcome House, High Street, Llandaff, Cardiff, is a comprehensive leaflet which carries a map; it tells you about the legal aspects and how to make enquiries concerning fishing facilities.

Eire

Fishing in conjunction with forest holidays is covered in *The Open Forest* from the Forest and Wildlife Service, 22 Upper Merrion Street, Dublin 2.

Northern Ireland

Game Fishing in Northern Ireland by Daniel McCrea and *Coarse Fishing in Northern Ireland* by Colin W. Graham are published by the Northern Ireland Tourist Board, River House, 48 High Street, Belfast BT1 2DS.

Deer Stalking and Trophy Hunting

A large number of private estates organise deer shoots for visitors, particularly in Scotland. Thirty-four such estates are listed in *Deer Stalking and Shooting* (from the Scottish Tourist Board, 23 Ravelston Terrace, Edinburgh EH4 3EU). Information includes fees charged, and whether keeper, gillie, beaters, dogs or rifles are supplied. The Forestry Commission (HQ for England, Scotland and Wales is: 231 Corstorphine Road, Edinburgh EH12 7AT) extends similar facilities on its land, as does the Forestry Division of the Department of Agriculture, Dundonald House, Upper Newtownards Road, Belfast BT4 3SB.

(Plate 12 overleaf) Fishing in Snowdonia Forest Park, North Wales *(Ronald Thompson)*

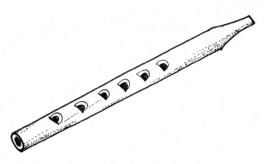

Fig 16 For making your own campfire music, elder (not alder) sticks are hollow and the pith can be pushed out with the tommy bar in the car tool kit or some similar metal rod – even with a wooden rod if carefully fashioned and smoothed – to provide a wooden tube. Cut notches in one side of the tube through to the hollow centre. A small hole makes a high note and a large one a low note. You will have to experiment to get it just right, so start with all small holes and gradually enlarge as required. Shape the mouthpiece and you have your forest-holiday flute!

In traditional deer stalking, the hunter normally has to be content with an allocation of quarries of about one good head in six, but he usually retains the carcasses (venison). In trophy hunting, a fairly modern version of the sport, in which good-headed quarries are exclusively or chiefly allocated, the successful hunter is assigned the head (generally mounted for him) as the trophy, but not customarily the venison. Trophy hunting is, understandably, by far the more expensive. The weapon used in both stalking and trophy hunting is a high-velocity rifle, between 256 and 303 calibre, with soft-nosed bullets.

A game licence, available from all main and branch post offices, is required, also a firearms certificate – obtainable at the police HQ of the area in which the applicant is *resident* – for the use of a rifle.

Closed seasons vary with species and sex. For particulars see the 'Complete' or 'Library' editions of *Whitaker's Almanack* under 'Game (Close Times)'. No species of deer may be taken from one hour after sunset to one hour before sunrise.

Landowners will seldom accept liability for injury or damage during shoots. Be sure to take out appropriate insurance cover beforehand.

For information on stalking and trophy hunting, write to The British Field Sports Society, 26 Caxton Street, London SW1H ORG.

Winged Game Shooting

The contents of a game bag varies widely from one part of the British Isles to another. Best pheasant shoots are in the sunnier, drier eastern areas, but good to average bags may be had in the west. Apart from climate, the quality of shoots alters from forest to forest, and prices vary accordingly. Mixed bags in England, Wales and Ireland will produce pheasant, woodcock, snipe, quail (in summer), wildfowl and wood pigeon; in Scotland, pheasant, wildfowl, blackgame (black grouse) and capercaillie. Red grouse and partridge are not woodland birds.

Capercaillie and blackgame (unlike red grouse) are not regarded very highly as delicacies, although they make a welcome addition to the table. A number of Scottish estates are therefore building up their pheasant stocks to provide good pheasant shoots (mainly in November and December) or attractive mixed shoots (often over a wider range of months). The Scottish Tourist Board leaflet, *Deer Stalking and Shooting*, will help you choose your game forest.

The Northern Ireland Tourist Board, 48 High Street, Belfast BTI 2DS maintains a list of estate owners' addresses and shooting terms in Ulster. For other parts of the British Isles, apply direct to the individual estate.

Close seasons for the various species of game birds are given under 'Game (Close Times)' in the 'Complete' and 'Library' editions of *Whitaker's Almanack*.

A shotgun certificate, obtainable at the police HQ of the area in which the applicant is *resident*, is required, also a game licence, obtainable at all main and branch post offices.

Landowners will seldom accept liability for injury or damage during shoots. Be sure to take out appropriate insurance cover beforehand.

2 Cultural Activities

Painting and Sketching

With their infinite variety of ever-changing patterns and colours, and abundance of wildlife forms, the forests of the British Isles provide unlimited subjects for the amateur and professional artist – whether one's medium be oil, water colour, pen, pencil, ink or tempera, now coming back into vogue. Another method gaining in popularity is to photograph the subject in the woods and then paint it back home – a particularly useful device when painting an animal, bird or insect. Reluctant still-life sitters, they can be captured in every minute detail by the speed and accuracy of a good colour camera.

You can build up an interesting and instructive portfolio of sketches or paintings by taking the same subject at different seasons of the year; a beechwood, for example, with its pale greens of spring, the more sombre greens of summer, the russets and golds of autumn, and the bare silver-grey branches of winter. Or you can do a series of then-and-now pictures; take a young forest – or even an individual tree – and paint or sketch it year by year as it develops.

All the best artists know that the more they understand about the subject the better will be their chance of producing worthwhile work. (Pages 100 to 102 tell you how to improve your knowledge of woodland wildlife.) For anyone wanting to learn more about the techniques of painting and sketching, RVS Enterprises, Hilton House, Norwood Lane, Meopham, Kent DA13 0YE, run courses in art, lasting from two to seven days. A brochure will be sent on application. Apply also to the Educational Development Association, 8 Windmill Gardens, Enfield, Middlesex EN2 7DU for information about their summer schools; minimum age of students, 18 years.

Photography and Sound Recording

Photography, like painting, can be practised anywhere, but at some forests nature hides have been erected, which can be used for taking

(*Plate 13 opposite*) Rock climbing in the Cairngorms. But get some tuition (see page 85) before you try anything like this (*B.H. Humble*)

photographs of wildlife. A nature hide is an observation platform which is mounted either above or at ground level on an appropriate vantage point.

Many photographer-naturalists, however, prefer to stalk and take shots of wildlife without the aid of a hide; not wanting to have their scope restricted in this way, they like to seek out their own subjects wherever these may be found. This is known as photo-safari. Even those who are less competent can, at certain forests, benefit from the services of an informed guide on safari.

A charge is usually made for admission to a hide and always for the services of a guide on safari. Grisedale Forest in the Lake District extends special facilities to photographers, both in respect of hides and photo-safaris. Apply to the Chief Forester, Forestry Commission, Grisedale Forest, Ambleside, Cumbria.

There is a wide range of markets for photographs of wildlife. See 'Markets for Photographers' in *The Writers' and Artists' Year Book*, published by A & C Black.

When on safari, take with you a portable tape recorder. The long waits between shots can gainfully be employed by recording bird song and other sounds of the forest that will really bring your holiday back to life on long winter evenings.

Studying Wildlife

There is no better place for the study of wildlife than a food-filled forest. No other kind of habitat has such a wide range of insect, bird and animal species – and plant species, too.

And there is no better way for the novice to begin his studies than by following a woodland nature trail with brochure in hand. The brochure will tell him just what to look for at each stage on the route, give a broad idea of the various branches of study and show how they hang together. Such a practical initiation will also do much to enhance his powers of observation.

Nature trails are marked on the touring maps published by the tourist boards for Scotland and Wales. The English Tourist Board publishes a list of nature trails in England. Forest nature trails are given in *See Your Forests* – in four parts: *Northern England, Southern England, Scotland, Wales* – published by the Forestry Commission. For Eire, the forest park guides and other literature of the Forest and Wildlife

Service carry nature trails. For Northern Ireland, apply to the Forestry Division of the Department of Agriculture.

For keys to deeper study, refer to the Forestry Commission's *Catalogue of Publications* which lists not only the forest park and forest guides, containing much valuable information on all aspects of wildlife in the woodlands covered, but includes numerous well-illustrated and informative booklets and leaflets on plant, insect, bird and animal life of the British woodlands. See also:

Scotland for the Birdwatcher, Scottish Tourist Board.

Bird Watching in Northern Ireland, and

Familiar Flowers of Northern Ireland, Northern Ireland Tourist Board.

Some Irish Bird Haunts, Forest and Wildlife Service, Eire.

Your local (public) librarian will be pleased to indicate to you, and procure for you, the most appropriate books and papers on any branch of wildlife study in which you are interested, consonant with the standard you have reached. The public libraries also have an information service – not widely known – under which, if in their power, they will supply the answer to any serious question on any subject.

Regarding tuition, the Field Studies Council organise one-week holidays in their numerous field study centres. Each provides a full range of courses covering such subjects as birds, ecology and conservation. The National Institute of Adult Education publishes a six-monthly list of residential short courses held at colleges of adult education throughout the country. Write to either for further particulars.

Records of bird songs and animal cries may be purchased from most music shops, also sometimes from the record departments of multiple stores or from the Society for the Promotion of Nature Reserves.

Addresses of organisations referred to above:

English Tourist Board, 4 Grosvenor Gardens, London SW1W ODU.

Field Studies Council, 9 Devereux Court, Strand, London WC2R 3JR.

Forestry Commission, 231 Corstorphine Road, Edinburgh EH12 7AT.

Forestry Division, Department of Agriculture, Dundonald House, Upper Newtownards Road, Belfast BT4 3SB.

Forest and Wildlife Service, 22 Upper Merrion Street, Dublin 2, Eire.

National Institute of Adult Education, 35 Queen Anne Street, London WIM OBL.

Northern Ireland Tourist Board, 48 High Street, Belfast BTI 2DS.

Scottish Tourist Board, 23 Ravelston Terrace, Edinburgh EII4 3EU.

Society for the Promotion of Nature Reserves, The Green, Nettleham, Lincoln.

Wales Tourist Board, High Street, Llandaff, Cardiff.

PART C

Choosing Your Accommodation

Introduction

Forest holidays in the British Isles – with the scope and on the scale in which they are available today – have only been made possible by the large tree-planting programmes carried out since the war. And, as forests need to be at least twenty-five years old before they become suitable for recreation, many are just coming in. Some owners have been quicker than others to realise the recreational potential of their woodlands and have been speedier off the mark. There are also those who adhere to a policy of reserving their forests for the growing of timber and for their own pleasure. However, all three state forest authorities have positive programmes for recreational development. Since most recreational facilities are easier, quicker and cheaper to

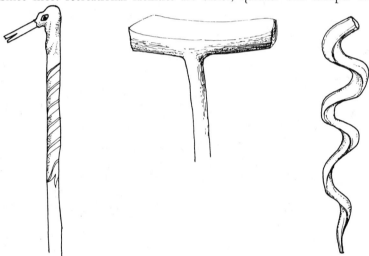

Fig 17 A walking stick or shooting stick can be a useful item. With permission, pull up (do *not* cut off) a young sapling of ash, birch or hazel. The root becomes the grip or handle and can often be fashioned into interesting shapes

Ivy stems can be found in old woodlands which are thick enough to make walking sticks, or even shooting sticks (to take your weight). Shooting sticks can also be made from a branch with the half section of the trunk attached, the half section of the trunk being fashioned into a seat. Ash, oak, birch and sycamore are useful for this purpose

Children (of all ages) will go for this one. Used by the old music hall comedians it is made from honeysuckle which has been carefully parted from the tree trunk it constricted. A neglected larch wood is about the best place to look for this

provide than most forms of overnight accommodation, there are still many instances, particularly in privately owned forests, where this is not laid on.

Even so, 'in-forest accommodation' (see following Chapter 1) is not at all hard to come by when one knows how and where to look; and it is the purpose of Chapter 2 to show just that. In 1975, for example, the Forestry Commission had in-forest accommodation for nearly 5,000 family units; taking the main holiday season as being from mid-May to mid-September, this means an intake capacity of well over 80,000 families if each stayed for one week during that period. Substantial additional accommodation is being built – by the Commission and others – and plans for further expansion are already in the pipeline.

It is not enough, however, merely to know how to find accommodation. You need to find out whether it is suited to the type of forest holiday you have in mind. Chapter 1 helps you here.

1 Range and Suitability of Accommodation

Availability

Forest-holiday accommodation comes under two broad headings: 'in-forest' and 'near-forest' accommodation. 'In-forest accommodation' covers overnight accommodation of any kind within the forest boundary, either among the trees or around the perimeter. 'Near-forest accommodation' signifies overnight accommodation within view, or within easy reach, of the holiday forest.

In-forest accommodation

This includes camping and caravan sites, chalet holiday centres, forest log cabin holiday centres, furnished holiday cottages or lodges, and cottages, occupied by forestry workers and others, which cater for visitors – to the extent of providing bed and board and perhaps an evening meal.

Not all these come under the forest owner. For example, he will not normally be concerned with the bed-and-breakfast traffic of his tenants, or he may have leased the caravan and camping site to a private company. Consequently, it is sometimes necessary to make separate bookings for overnight accommodation and for recreational or sporting facilities, such as permits for deer stalking, shooting and fishing, or the hiring of mounts. But this would be the exception rather than the rule.

Near-forest accommodation

The wide range includes hotels, motels, hostels, historic country houses, guesthouses, furnished cottages and flats, boarding houses, farmhouses, caravan and camping grounds, holiday chalets. Very few, if any, of these will come under the control of the forest owner or authority.

Forest park accommodation

In a separate category are the forest parks of England, Scotland and Wales. These are made up of groups of forests with perhaps mountains, moorland, farmland – and even villages and small towns – in between which, *in toto*, make an attractive forest holiday resort. The hotels, motels, hostels, etc, in these forest parks are therefore, in a very real sense, part of the in-forest accommodation. This is also, to some degree, true of some other large groups of forests – such as Thetford Chase in Norfolk/Suffolk and the Allerston Forest of north-east Yorkshire – which are not, or not as yet, designated forest parks. The forest parks of both Northern and Southern Ireland can be considered, for accommodation purposes, as single forests.

Suitability
Individual preference

Coming to a decision on the type of accommodation in which to stay depends upon a number of things – the first, obviously, being whether it is available at the holiday forest of your choice. With the forest parks of England, Scotland and Wales, there is no problem. Elsewhere, for certain kinds of forest holidays, it might sometimes even prove more satisfactory to fit the forest to the accommodation rather than the other way around. For example, if you and your family are keen campers, owning a full range of camping equipment, it will be important for you to find a holiday forest which has a good campsite. The overwhelming majority have, but there are a few exceptions.

On the other hand, if a member of your party is aged or infirm, camping – or even caravanning – is unlikely to suit them. They will probably need a room of their own and may be restricted in the distance they are able to walk. If you book into some nearby hotel or guesthouse – unless it lies in a forest park and affords panoramic views of woodlands – the only glimpse they may get of the trees is through the car window, providing you have a car. The ideal choice for those who are less mobile would be a forest log cabin or a woodland chalet where they have only to step out on to the verandah to see the woods and wildlife all around them.

Forest log cabins are particularly appropriate for the kind of holiday where you want to get right away and relax without sacrificing too many amenities and comforts, even though you do your own catering, cooking and cleaning. They are also well suited to certain activity or cultural holidays. For instance, supposing your main interests are natural history and photography, those of your wife painting and sketching, while your eldest son wants some sport with a gun and your younger children are keen on riding. That means a great deal of equipment to store away safely without it getting damp or wet. A tent is unsuitable, a caravan would be too cluttered up, and to pack it all into a car each morning at a nearby hotel and transport it to the woods, reversing the whole process at night, would hardly add to the pleasure of the holiday. Yet, in such an admittedly extreme case, this might have to be done, as the number of forest cabins available is still strictly limited.

Then, there is the forest holidaymaker for whom camping has no appeal, yet whose purse is not long enough to run to serviced accommodation, such as hotels and guesthouses, or even to unserviced accommodation like log cabins. Here I would suggest either a youth hostel (contrary to what the name implies, there is no upper or lower age limit) or bed and breakfast with evening meal at a forest worker's or keeper's cottage. The snag is that these cottages do not show up in any of the accommodation guides; and estate or forest offices do not handle such bookings, although they might be able and willing to put anyone interested in touch with a forest worker so that he could make his own arrangements.

Many a keeper's or forest worker's cottage is ensconced well within the forest boundary where the true tang of the woods may be experienced. Others stand at forest entrances. Any of these provide a good operational base for the naturalist or the hunter, and for his equipment. And there is no better way of getting inside information about the woods than sleeping under the roof and sitting at the table of someone whose way of life they are.

For the real loner it is often possible to get the owner's permission to pitch your tent or park your caravan at a place other than a prepared campsite – somewhere deep in the woods. This should be a particularly attractive arrangement for nature lovers and students. But it is essential strictly to observe any conditions which the owner might impose, especially with regard to the lighting of fires and not disturbing nests and game, and other wildlife.

Many farms have common boundaries with forests and a number lie within the borders of forest parks in England, Scotland and Wales. There are numerous farmhouses, and not a few farm cottages, which offer very good board and lodging in forest areas. Even so, and without

(Plate 14) A member and his family in one of the woods in the Countryside Club scheme. There are over 50 woodlands from which to choose. For particulars write to: The Countryside Club, 109 Upper Woodcote Road, Caversham Heights, Reading RG4 7LA *(The Countryside Club)*

any prejudice against the farming community, I am somewhat hesitant to recommend them to those seeking a forest holiday; for, although forestry and farming have a great deal in common, they are nevertheless two distinct ways of life. Staying on a farm, with its own very real and particular attractions, cannot help but detract in some measure from the forest holiday atmosphere. Hotels, motels, guesthouses and other types of near-forest accommodation are neutral in this respect; farmhouse or farm cottage accommodation is not. On the other hand, for those seeking a 'country' holiday, as opposed to a specifically 'forest' or 'farm' holiday, such a combination could prove ideal.

For the holidaymaker with a more princely approach to forest activities, there are a number of historic country mansions which have been turned into hotels and still have their woodlands intact as part of the hotel grounds. A high proportion of these woods – and some are fairly extensive – are open to the paying guest for shooting or other purposes. Particulars of hotel woodlands are included in the Scottish Tourist Board leaflet, *Historic and Country House Hotels and Inns in Scotland* (see page 121), but such information is not given in the main accommodation guides where country house hotels in the rest of the British Isles are listed.

Appropriate to holiday activity

Walking and climbing. The best types of accommodation for walkers and climbers are campsites and hostels, the great advantage being that very many of these are remote from towns and villages and located well up into the kind of terrain where these activities may be enjoyed. What is more, the right sort of atmosphere is created from the moment you drop your rucksack by the side of the hostel bed or pitch your tent.

Riding. It may not be generally known that a number of riding establishments provide accommodation for visitors. Many of these, particularly those in the forest parks, are well situated amid woodland and other good riding country. Such surroundings are also conducive to the right kind of atmosphere for the keen horseman on a forest holiday.

Ski-ing. Despite the fact that ski-ing on snow can only be enjoyed during the colder months of the year, there are campsites open for the benefit of skiers. These would mainly attract the young and the hardy, and a good-quality sleeping-bag would be an essential item of camping

Fig 18 When finding your way back on a non-waymarked trail, do not trailblaze (ie, cut slivers of bark from tree trunks). It's like slicing off a piece of your skin. Disease can get in. Foresters in Britain only blaze trees that are to be felled
In addition to enabling you to find your way back the two methods shown above will also tell others the way you have gone. But, if you don't want them to know, simply place a pile of stones, or push a stick into the ground, at the end of the track you are *leaving*

equipment. Most potential skiers would be much more comfortable in a hostel or hotel in the vicinity of the ski slopes.

Sailing. Numerous campsites, hostels and hotels are to be found around the shores of lochs and lakes in holiday forest areas, some almost at the water's edge. A fair proportion have good mooring arrangements but not so many provide suitable launching facilities for the larger sailing craft and cabin cruisers. Check on these matters when making preliminary enquiries. Also well represented are sailing schools and clubs and these, needless to say, all have excellent mooring and launching facilities. Some even have their own accommodation while others will be happy to arrange convenient local bookings or at least furnish the information. For particulars of schools and clubs consult the publications referred to under *Boating* in Part B (page 89).

Canoeing. Canoes are the most versatile watercrafts for use in the wilderness; they can negotiate narrows and shallows which a sailing boat cannot, and are portable over short stretches of land. On a canoe safari through forest areas, the tent is the ideal form of overnight accommodation; providing permission is forthcoming, it can be pitched on the bank of a river, lake or loch where the voyage ends for the day.

Fishing. Most fishing tackle can be stored in an average-sized tent;

this being so, it follows that all types of accommodation are suitable. The choice of billet therefore depends entirely on the fisherman's personal preference.

Game shooting. For anyone intent on shooting game while on a forest holiday during the open season, safari camping might well be frowned upon by the owners who insist that guns are kept away from woods at night. The weather at such times of the year also makes this type of accommodation unsuitable, particularly as cartridges need to be kept dry. A warm house, hotel or forest log cabin would be preferable.

Cultural activities. Your choice of accommodation will depend to some extent on whether you are planning to paint, take photographs or study wildlife; on the amount of equipment you need, and the time of year when you have your holiday. Camping and caravan sites are open all the year round in the Cairngorms, for example; in the Lake District they open one week before Easter until the end of October, and elsewhere generally close from mid-September to mid-April.

2 Selection of Accommodation

As the forest holiday industry in the British Isles, as elsewhere, is in such an active state of expansion it is important that the prospective forest holidaymaker should consult up-to-date accommodation guides in order to ascertain all that is currently available. While there is as yet no single accommodation guide embracing all the various kinds of forest-holiday overnight places to stay, no doubt this will come in time. Meanwhile, there are guides which cover the caravan and camping sites run by the Forestry Commission (covering England, Scotland and Wales) and those managed by the Forestry Division (Northern Ireland). For other forest caravan and camping sites, and for all other types of forest-holiday accommodation, you will need to consult the general accommodation guides in combination with maps and forest-holiday literature.

The information given below is set out in such a way as to be most helpful in this respect, being classified first by accommodation type and then by country. Where an organisation is mentioned only once in the text, its address immediately follows; in other cases, the addresses are listed at the end of the chapter.

Caravan and Campsites

Caravan and campsites differ widely in the facilities and services they offer. It is therefore very advisable to find out, at the time of making initial enquiries, exactly what these are, if not already stated in the literature. Some establishments, although describing themselves only as caravan parks or caravan sites, also have pitches set aside for tents. Again, there are several different kinds of caravan accommodation. Some establishments are for touring caravans only (stays are limited to one, two or a few nights). Others are set aside only for extended holiday stays, ranging from not less than seven to fourteen nights. A few do not accept visitors' caravans at all, their business being to hire out static (*in situ*) caravans. In very many cases, two or more of the above facilities are combined, while others will hire out mobile caravans, saving you the inconvenience of towing one over long distances to the holiday ground.

With regard to services, the most important point to bear in mind is that some establishments have no toilets and will only accept those caravans which carry their own closets. Tenters would not be welcomed at these places either, unless they, too, carry chemical closets.

Generally speaking, most establishments cater for both tents and caravans, for long and short stays, regardless of what gear or equipment is carried.

Northern Ireland

The Northern Ireland Tourist Board publishes a list of caravan and camping sites of which 30 out of a total of 90 lie either within or near forest areas. Number of spaces for touring caravans and tents is given where known; as are type of facilities available, such as dogs admitted, car parking beside caravan/tent, food shop, café/restaurant, etc. Centres with caravans for hire are also given.

The Forestry Division of the Department of Agriculture publishes annually a brochure, *Touring in the Trees*, which lists caravan sites only. Two types are listed: Forest Touring Caravan Sites, where the length of stay is restricted to three days on any one site; and Forest Caravan Sites, where the limitation of stay is 14 days. The Forest Touring Caravan Sites have only the basic essentials, such as drinking water, chemical disposal unit and hard standing for the caravan. Only caravans equipped with chemical toilets will be admitted to these sites, of which there are twenty-two. The Forest Caravan Sites – four in number – offer greater comforts and a wider range of amenities.

For camping (tenting) in the state forests apply direct to the Forestry Division of the Ministry of Agriculture for Northern Ireland.

While the tourist board's list gives caravan and camping sites on both state and private forests, the Forestry Division's brochure covers state forests only. On the other hand, not all the Forestry Division's caravan sites are included in the tourist board's list. You therefore need both the list and the brochure to get the full picture.

Many caravan and camping sites are shown on the *Tourist Map of Northern Ireland*, published by the Northern Ireland Tourist Board. A general map, and site maps, are included in *Touring in the Trees*.

Write to the National Trust in Northern Ireland, Malone House, Barnett's Demesne, Belfast 5PU BT9 for particulars of their woodland caravan and camping sites.

Eire

There is no published information specifically relating to forest caravan and camping sites in Eire. However, the excellent booklet, *The Open Forest*, by the Forest and Wildlife Service, lists 300 forest areas (with facilities and holiday activities), including seven forest parks; and the Irish Tourist Board publishes an informative booklet, *Caravan and Camping Parks*, giving the area of each park, number of caravans to let on site, number of pitches available for tents, and range of amenities. A substantial proportion of these are within easy reach of one or more of the forest areas listed in *The Open Forest*. With the aid of a good map there will be no difficulty in relating the one to the other.

England

Forestry Commission campsites (caravans and/or tents) are given in the following leaflets:

> *Forestry Commission Campsites*
> *See Your Forests (Southern England)*
> *See Your Forests (Northern England)*

They are also shown on their *Guide Map to Your Forests*.

Forestry Commission campsites are divided into three classes: A, B and Woodland Sites. Class A sites are equipped with flush lavatories and hot and cold showers. They are supervised by a full-time resident warden and there is usually a shop on the site. Class B sites and Woodland Sites have a minimum of facilities and are designed for the camper with his own toilet (ie not suitable for tenters). They have chemical disposal points and water (potable) points only. Class A and Class B sites are usually on open ground (eg in a clearing or on the forest edge), but Woodland Sites have their pitches in among the trees. Dogs are admitted to all sites but must be kept on lead within the camp.

Camps are normally open from 1 April (or Easter, if earlier) to 30 September; some of them have an extended period of opening. Very few sites accept bookings in advance, except at bank holiday periods, when an additional booking fee is charged. Space is otherwise usually available, but at peak holiday times it is advisable to arrive early in the day.

The Lake District, Peak and Exmoor National Parks all publish lists of campsites, many of them close to forests and woodlands. See also, *Accommodation in the Yorkshire Dales* – which includes caravan and camping sites – issued by The Yorkshire Dales Tourist Association, Dept 47, Burnsall via Skipton, Yorkshire, BD23 6BP.

The National Trust has its own forests and woodlands. Write to them for information and for their list, *National Trust Camping and Caravan Sites*.

There are, as yet, few campsites in privately owned forests in England and there is no published list. However, a number of private-woodland owners will permit camping or caravanning on their land if approached directly. See also:

AA Guide to Camping and Caravanning. Over 300 pages with nearly 1,000 approved sites in Britain, location maps and list of all-the-year-round campsites.

Camping Sites in Britain, Link House Publications Ltd, Dingwall Avenue, Croydon, Surrey CR9 2TA.

Camping and Caravan Sites, British Travel Association.

Wales

Forestry Commission campsites (caravans and/or tents) are given in the following leaflets:

Forestry Commission Campsites
See Your Forests (*Wales*)

They also appear on their *Guide Map to Your Forests*.

The notes on Forestry Commission campsites under *England* (above) also apply to Wales.

The National Trust has its own forests and woodlands. Write for information and their list, *National Trust Camping and Caravan Sites*.

The tourist map, published by the Wales Tourist Board, shows forest picnic sites and nature trails, but does not mark campsites. It does show Forestry Commission information centres (as does *Guide Map to Your Forests*); enquire at one of these if you live, or are travelling, in the area.

As far as I have been able to discover, no forest under private ownership in Wales has set up a caravan or camping site, but it is likely that a number of owners would be willing to grant permission if approached directly.

See also:

AA Guide to Camping and Caravanning. Lists nearly 1,000 approved sites in Britain. Location maps and list of all-the-year-round camp-sites.

Camping Sites in Britain, Link House Publications Ltd, Dingwall Avenue, Croydon CR9 2TA.

Camping and Caravan Sites, British Travel Association.

Scotland

Forestry Commission campsites (caravans and/or tents) are given in the following leaflets:

Forestry Commission Campsites

See Your Forests (Scotland)

They also appear on their *Guide Map to Your Forests*.

The notes on Forestry Commission campsites under *England* (page 115) also apply to Scotland.

The Scottish Tourist Board publishes an excellent 86-page hand-book, *Scotland for Touring Caravans*. Its coverage is wider than the name implies, catering for the caravanner, the motor caravanner and the tenter. Well over 400 sites are listed, which between them provide more than 1,600 pitches for touring outfits, very many of them either within or close to forests. In the handbook, each site carries a map reference number and can thus be identified on one of the location maps in the centre pages. These maps do not, however, show forest areas, so it is necessary to use them in conjunction with the *Scotland Touring Map* (Scottish Tourist Board); this shows the forest areas, with their recreational amenities, but not campsites. The Forestry Commission's *Guide Map to Your Forests* shows only its own camp-sites.

Facilities and amenities of each campsite are given in symbol form in the *Scotland for Touring Caravans* handbook. Running water and toilet facilities are not stated as, under the Caravan Sites Act, 1960, these are compulsory for campsites in Scotland. The handbook does *not* include details of sites on which static (in situ) caravans are available for hire. These appear in the Scottish Tourist Board's publication, *Self Catering Accommodation in Scotland*. The majority of campsites in Scotland, particularly at peak periods, will accept advanced bookings.

See also:

Fig 19 In Britain's ancient forests, such as the New and the Dean, many foresters carry an umbrella in the woods

An umbrella can be useful for keeping off the rain and drips from leaves after it has stopped

You can prod for adders

Or test the firmness of the ground

You can even hook down wild fruits!

(Plate 15) Relaxing in a woodland chalet near Newton Stewart, Wigtownshire *(Conifer Leisure Park)*

AA Guide to Camping and Caravanning. Lists nearly 1,000 approved sites in Britain. Location maps and list of all-the-year-round campsites.

Camping Sites in Britain, Link House Publications Ltd, Dingwall Avenue, Croydon CR9 2TA.

Camping and Caravan Sites, British Travel Association.

Forest Cabins

The forest cabin, or log cabin – the very latest in forest-holiday accommodation in Britain – has been pioneered by the Forestry Commission, but private forestry interests are almost certain to adopt this concept in the near future. The first forest cabins to be erected and available for occupation are the seventeen on the shores of Loch Lubnaig, near Strathyre in Perthshire (for a description of their structure, furnishings and amenities, see Part A, Chapter 2). However, it is worth keeping a close eye on developments as a recent feasibility study indicates that the Forestry Commission possesses suitable sites for some 7,300 self-catering forest cabins – in clusters, as at Strathyre, or in small villages – and for eleven forest lodges. These lodges will be like hotels, but occupying in-forest settings; full service will be provided, plus the various facilities and amenities that go with a forest holiday.

For particulars of the forest cabins at Strathyre apply to the Forestry Commission, Portcullis House, 21 India Street, Glasgow G2 4PL.

Forest Holiday Cottages and Chalets

The National Trust has holiday cottages in Cornwall, Dorset, the Lake District and Northern Ireland. Some are situated in or near forests or woodlands. Apply to the National Trust for details.

The Forestry Commission has a number of forest holiday cottages in or near forests in England, Scotland and Wales. Make initial enquiries to their head office at 231 Corstorphine Road, Edinburgh EH12 7AT, stating geographical preference.

For other holiday cottages and chalets, see selected forest holidays in Part A; also refer to *Other Accommodation* (below).

Forest Workers' and Keepers' Cottages

As the forestry authorities do not undertake bookings for bed and breakfast accommodation in estate cottages, you will need to make your own arrangements direct – either through knowledge gained on a previous visit or through a contact in the area. With private forestry, some estates are prepared to pass on names and addresses to the enquirer. Bookings can then be negotiated by post with the employee or tenant of the cottage.

Other Accommodation

This includes hotels, motels, guesthouses, boarding houses, farmhouses, youth hostels, furnished cottages and flats, either within the boundaries of a forest park or within easy travelling distance of a holiday forest. The intending holidaymaker will need to consult forest holiday literature and maps, tourist and other maps, in conjunction with the following general accommodation guides:

Scotland

Where to Stay in Scotland. Over 380 pages. The National (ie Scottish) Register of Accommodation, published by the Scottish Tourist Board. It contains registers of hotels, guesthouses, farmhouse accommodation and youth hostels, and is divided into seven regions. It includes a sectional map supplement, a list of tourist information centres and much valuable general information.

AA Guide to Hotels and Restaurants in Great Britain. Includes motels as well. About 90 pages refer to Scotland. There is a section on the Scottish mainland and another on Scottish islands, some of which support forests. It contains a set of location maps and much useful general information.

Accommodation Guide Grampian Region, published by the Grampian Tourist Association, 17 High Street, Elgin IV30 IEG. 32 pages. Includes hotels, motels, guesthouses, bed and breakfast premises, self-catering accommodation (cottages, flats, chalets), caravans to let (static), caravan and camping sites.

Central Scotland Holiday Accommodation Guide (ie Stirlingshire, Clackmannanshire, West Perthshire), published by the Central Scotland Tourist Association, County Offices, Viewforth, Stirling FK8 2ET. 40 pages. Includes hotels, guesthouses, farmhouses, bed and breakfast premises, furnished cottages and flats, chalets, caravans to let (static), caravan and camping sites.

Then, there are the specialised accommodation guides – those dealing with a particular kind of accommodation:

Self Catering Accommodation in Scotland, published by the Scottish Tourist Board. 90 pages. Includes furnished cottages and flats, chalets, caravans for hire (static and towing). Highly informative concerning facilities and amenities.

Motels in Scotland, published by the Scottish Tourist Board. Four-page leaflet. The 35 motels listed all appear in *Where to Stay in Scotland* but, for anyone who has decided on this type of accommodation, it saves purchasing the main guide.

Hotels with Swimming Pools and Golf Courses, published by the Scottish Tourist Board. The 56 hotels listed in this four-page leaflet also appear in the National Register, *Where to Stay in Scotland*.

Historic and Country House Hotels and Inns in Scotland, published by the Scottish Tourist Board. 24 pages. Although the establishments listed are also included in the main guide, *Where to Stay in Scotland*, only this leaflet gives particulars of the woodlands attached to them (see page 110), with the sporting facilities, such as fishing or shooting, which are available.

Wales

Where to Stay in Wales, published by the Wales Tourist Board. 200 pages. Includes hotels, motels, inns, guesthouses, farmhouse accommodation, caravan and camping sites, furnished cottages and flats, and youth hostels. Has a one-page map of Wales inside the front cover, but no sectional or location maps. The Wales Tourist Board also publishes a very good 1 in tourist map which needs to be used in conjunction with the guide.

AA Guide to Hotels and Restaurants in Great Britain. Also includes motels. Information is given under the England and Wales' section of the guide. Counties are clearly indicated. Contains a set of location maps and much useful general information.

Wales has three national parks: Snowdonia, Brecon Beacons, and Pembrokeshire Coast. These contain many areas of highly scenic forest and woodland. Each national park issues its own accommodation guide and lists. Addresses at the end of this chapter.

England

Where to Stay in . . . This is a series of eleven official accommodation guides published by the English Tourist Board and covering the whole of England, region by region. For example, *Where to Stay in the West Country*, the largest of all the guides, runs to 120 pages. Others in the series are: English Lakeland; Northumbria; North West England; Yorkshire, Cleveland and Humberside; Heart of England; English Shires; Thames and Chilterns; East Anglia; London; South East England; Hampshire, East Dorset and the Isle of Wight. The whole series, totalling almost 1,000 pages, constitutes the biggest guide yet issued for the holidaymaker in England. All forms of accommodation are listed: hotels, motels, guesthouses and other serviced establishments; self-catering accommodation (chalets, static caravan sites, furnished cottages, bungalows, flats and flatlets); camping and caravan sites; holiday camps, and accommodation for groups and young people – a number of riding premises are entered here. A comprehensive symbols code indicates facilities and amenities, and there is a grid map indexed to place names.

Let's Go, published by the English Tourist Board. Lists over 600 hotels offering reduced week-end (and some mid-week) rates for out-of-season holidays. This guide is particularly useful for the forest holidaymaker planning a few days fishing or shooting – or just relaxing.

AA Guide to Hotels and Restaurants in Great Britain. Also includes motels. Information listed in the guide under 'England and Wales'. Counties are clearly indicated. Contains a set of location maps and much useful general information.

England has seven national parks: Peak District, Lake District, Dartmoor, North York Moors, Yorkshire Dales, Exmoor, and Northumberland. These contain many acres of highly scenic forest and woodland. Each national park issues its own accommodation guide and lists. Addresses at the end of this chapter.

Northern Ireland

Northern Ireland. All the Places to Stay. Published by the Northern Ireland Tourist Board. 34 pages. Includes hotels, guesthouses, farm and country house accommodation. Each establishment is given a grid reference letter and number which corresponds with a place on the location map on the back of the guide. Facilities and amenities are shown by symbols, ranging from acceptance of dogs, swimming pool, boating and sailing, availability of fishing and game shooting, to riding, sketching and painting instruction.

Southern Ireland

Hotels, Guesthouses in Ireland. Sent free of charge to addresses *outside* Eire. This is the official guide published by the Irish Tourist Board. 46 pages. Each establishment is given a grid reference letter and number which corresponds with a place on the location map in the guide. Motor hotels are also listed and are generally found on or near trunk roads. Unlike other hotels, meal services in these may be limited. Information includes babysitter services, central heating, swimming pools.

Town and Country Homes, Farmhouses in Ireland. 54 pages. Published by the Irish Tourist Board and complementary to the official guide. Information particularly useful to forest holidaymakers on fishing and riding, and whether the establishment is in a rural setting.

Holidays and Weekends in our Hostels. Leaflet published by An Óige, 39 Mountjoy Square, Dublin 1. Includes a list of hostels and details of conditions and charges. The *Map of Ireland*, published by the Irish Tourist Board, makes a special feature of indicating the geographical position of these hostels.

Rent-an-Irish-Cottage Ltd (Shannon Free Airport, County Clare) has built a series of most attractive thatched-cottage villages. Write to them for particulars and for their location map and site plans.

The eight Regional Tourism Organisations issue their own accommodation lists in quantities limited to the number of premises available for renting. Write in the first instance to the Northern Ireland Tourist Board for their literature, plus a list of addresses of these regional organisations.

Addresses not included above

Automobile Association (AA), Fanum House, Basingstoke, Hampshire RG21 2EA.

English Tourist Board, 4 Grosvenor Gardens, London SW1W 0DU.

Forest and Wildlife Service, Department of Lands, 22 Upper Merrion Street, Dublin 2, Eire.

Forestry Commission (Headquarters for England, Scotland and Wales), 231 Corstorphine Road, Edinburgh EH12 7AT.

Forestry Division, Department of Agriculture, Dundonald House, Upper Newtownards Road, Belfast BT4 3SB.

Irish Tourist Board, Box 273, 63–67 Upper Stephen Street, Dublin 8, Eire.

National Parks (England)
Dartmoor: Devon County Council, County Hall, Exeter, Devon EX2 4QA
Exmoor: Market House, The Parade, Minehead, Somerset TA24 5NB
Lake District: Bank House, High Street, Windermere, Cumbria
North York Moors: County Hall, Northallerton DL7 8AD
Northumberland: County Planning Office, County Hall, Newcastle-upon-Tyne 1.
Peak District: Peak Park Planning Board, The National Park Office, Baslow Road, Bakewell, Derbyshire DE4 1AE
Yorkshire Dales: Yorebridge House, Bainbridge, Leyburn, North Yorkshire DL8 3BP

National Parks (Wales)
Brecon Beacons: Glamorgan Street, Brecon LD3 7DP.

Pembrokeshire Coast: County Museum, Haverfordwest Castle, Haverfordwest, Pembrokeshire.

Snowdonia: Yr Hen Ysgol, Maentwrog, Blaenau Ffestiniog, Merioneth LL41 4HW.

National Trust, 42 Queen Anne's Gate, London SW1H 9AS

National Trust for Northern Ireland, Malone House, Barnett's Demesne, Belfast BT9 5PU

National Trust for Scotland, 5 Charlotte Square, Edinburgh EH2 4DU

Northern Ireland Tourist Board, River House, 48 High Street, Belfast BT1 2DS

Scottish Tourist Board, 23 Ravelston Terrace, Edinburgh EH4 3EU

Wales Tourist Board, Welcome House, High Street, Llandaff, Cardiff CF5 2YZ

Appendix: Hire and Purchase of Equipment

The names and addresses of suppliers of caravans for towing, motorised caravans and activity-holiday equipment, for sale or for hire, are too numerous to list here, but can be found in the trade sections of telephone directories – full sets of which are kept at main post offices. The following information may prove helpful in obtaining certain items from specialist sources.

Camping Equipment

Write to Blacks of Greenock (address: Port Glasgow, Renfrewshire PA14 5XN; and Ruxley Corner, Sidcup, Kent DA14 5AQ) for details of their camp-hire service centres in various parts of Britain.

Boats and Boating Equipment

Boat hire

Write for free brochure to Boat Enquiries Ltd, 7 Walton Well Road, Oxford.

Rowing, sailing and outboard boats, and buoyancy jackets

For hire from Borro Boats, Duncraggan Road, Oban, Argyllshire.

Inflatable watercraft

Sold by Department EH, C-Craft Inflatable Products Ltd, Kirkpatrick Mill, Atherton Road, Hindley Green, Wigan, Lancashire.

Skis and Skiwear

Write for free leaflet on hiring ski kit from Cairngorm Sports Development Ltd, 26 Church Street, Inverness. For sale or hire: from Blacks of Greenock (address above).

Skiwear for sale or hire

From Moss Bros (various branches); or from Sportique Leisurewear, 31 Broomfield Road, Chelmsford, Essex.

Grass skis

From Grilson Grass Skis Ltd, Badger's Holt, Marley Lane, Haslemere, Surrey GU27 3PZ.

Riding Kit

Riding clothes and equipment can be bought or hired from stock at Moss Bros, Bedford Street, Covent Garden, London; or, if given a few days' notice, from their other branches.

Maps

Ordnance Survey, Romsey Road, Maybush, Southampton SO9 4DU, issues a free catalogue giving details of all maps published by them.

Index